THE TAX INDUSTRY

is on a

CRA$H COUR$E

49 SHORTCUT STRATEGIES

To MAKING MORE MONEY **Now**
(WHILE YOU STILL CAN)

CHAUNCEY HUTTER, JR.

BEST-SELLING AUTHOR OF
"BLOCKBuster: How to Build a
Million Dollar Tax Business"

Copyright Notice

Disclaimer and/or Legal Notices

TABLE OF CONTENTS

TABLE OF CONTENTS

TABLE OF CONTENTS

TABLE OF CONTENTS

TABLE OF CONTENTS

Effective Multi-Layered Marketing Plan Lands Tax Pro Extra $23,000 In Profit

"Chauncey has given me a clear roadmap on how to put together an effective multi-layered marketing plan. Using his promotional methods, I put an extra $23,000 in the bank during tax season. The future looks bright and my profits are increasing!"

Scott Rulon
Rulon Financial & Tax

CPA Increases Sales By 80% In One Tax Season

"Chauncey helped me increase my gross sales by 80% in one tax season. His tax business ads have worked like crazy for over 10 years. There is no way that I would go back to the old "professional" way of marketing my tax business. It's scary to think where my practice would be now without Chauncey's help."

Carletta M. Price, CPA, CGMA, CERC

Marketing, Profit-Strategies and Management
Keys To Tax Biz Owner's Success

"Chauncey Hutter, Jr's expertise in Direct Marketing, Profit Generating Strategies and Business Management Common sense are the reasons why I pay attention to everything he says and do what I can to model his tax business success in my company."

Harrison Ulloa
Affirm Tax & Multi Service LLC

Tax Practice Up Over $47,000 And CPA Not
Even Halfway Through Tax Season

"I was satisfied with my level of sales, but to increase my profit I would try to cut every expense to the bone. In the process, I had painted myself into a corner ... working all the time and not getting paid for administrative related year-round services.

Chauncey told me to re-test some old ads I thought didn't work, but this time using his style of marketing. These updated marketing campaigns kicked butt compared to everything else I'd tried in the past.

I'm not even half way through this tax season and my tax practice is already up over $47,000 compared to last year!"

Peter D. Arnold, CPA

Chauncey's Personal CRASH …

It was Friday night, March 31st, my mom's 77th birthday. We just finished blowing out the candles at my parent's house when the phone call came.

"Why are you not in the hospital … did you see the test results?" my cardio doctor asked with a frustrated tone.

I said, "No, the stress test nurses sent me home."

"Well, your heart has blockages in five different areas … I'm in the process of finding you a bed in the hospital right now."

"Tonight?" I asked. "How about after the weekend? I could check myself in on Monday once my wife returns from her out-of-town trip."

"Did you notice your blood pressure dropped 65 points after three minutes on a treadmill? Didn't you feel extremely dizzy … I'm shocked you didn't pass out!" the doctor exclaimed.

"Sorry Mr. Hutter, but staying home this weekend is too risky. We must get you to a place where we can monitor your heart 24/7."

My brother-in-law drove me a short distance to the University of Virginia hospital and dropped me off before visiting hours were over that night. The only problem was, I was not visiting. I spent the next 15 days in this hospital "hotel" that felt like a prison.

Now don't get me wrong.

I'm EXTREMELY thankful a persistent nurse practitioner would not take "No" for an answer and kindly, but sternly encouraged me NOT to leave town to be a chaperon on my daughter's high school trip a couple days earlier. I finally agreed to take the stress test sooner rather than later, and thank God I did.

I was a heart attack or a stroke just waiting to happen.

But instead, no major episode happened. Severe damage to my body or mind averted.

Failing the stress test was the best thing that could have happened to me. Because a couple of days later, the doctors went in and got a closer look at my arteries and determined very quickly I needed heart surgery.

Triple Bypass Heart Surgery Saves Chauncey Hutter, Jr From A Personal Crash Course

After several baseline tests to determine the best strategy for moving forward, the expert heart surgeons did what they are trained to do. They took my heart out of my body, added three bypasses, put my ticker back in its place and started it back up again.

True transformation.

The lead surgeon told me the next day, everything went great … "you're good for another 40 years now."

"Now let the healing process begin. In several months, you'll feel better than ever!"

So, here's the lesson I want you to get …

I was walking around doing life and did not realize the seriousness of the hour I was living in.

Yes, I did feel some symptoms. I couldn't breathe as well as I used to. But when I showed up to my regular cardio check-ups, I always told the doctors I wasn't feeling any pain in my chest. (Because I wasn't.) My symptoms were a little different than normal.

Personally, I knew something was not quite right. But I never would have guessed my arteries were over 80% blocked in five separate locations in my heart.

I was on a Personal Crash Course.

Now, let's compare my personal encounter with walking up to the edge of a cliff and not stepping off, to the current situation we all face in the tax industry.

THE TAX INDUSTRY IS ON A CRASH COURSE.

Most tax business owners will deny this fact. However, many tax pros I talk with face-to-face will admit there are symptoms. Storm clouds have drifted over the mountain and are now in sight of their tax practice.

The commoditization of the tax industry is real.

This rampant poison to a tax professional's livelihood should give you all the information you need to know about the radical changes coming to the tax industry. Combine this with the never-ceasing technology growth, and we have a perfect storm on our hands.

Artificial Intelligence (AI) is not something new.

AI technology has impacted your life for many years. Maybe you just didn't recognize it as such. But now, you can't deny AI because this technology has broken into the tax industry. So much so, that the brand name of the tax industry began openly advertising their services using AI in 2017.

Did you see the Super Bowl commercial when H & R Block announced they were partnering with IBM and Watson (AI robot) to provide the "perfectly prepared" tax return?

Something I thought we would see at the retail level by 2020, has injected itself into everyday taxpayers' lives. As such, this shift in our industry must be dealt with now, not later.

What Should A Professional Tax Practitioner Do Now?

The obvious question moving forward is, "OK, but now what ... what do I do?"

As a tax business owner, how does one take the information that's been presented to me and move forward in a way that will work out best for me and my tax practice? Because, bottom line, preparing tax returns is what I do and this is how I put food on the table.

Are you saying the tax industry will get wiped out?

Absolutely not!

What I am saying is the tax industry is about to make a huge pivot. And what you do over the next several years (or don't do) will have significant consequences to your life.

Your greatest asset is not your tax prep skills. It's not your office location and for sure it's not your logo. No, the greatest asset you possess is your RELATIONSHIP you have with your clients. They trust you. They depend on your advice. They will listen and follow your lead because of your recommendation.

If tax preparation is in a downward spiral and your core service looks, feels and acts like a "commodity duck" ... then don't try and fight this unwinnable battle. If you keep doing what you've always done, you will lose. Tax prep services are racing to the bottom of the fee scale and you don't want to be in that business -- only.

The main advice I want to give you is this:

You have two options and several strategies which go hand in hand with each. Personally, I recommend you DO BOTH options in your tax business.

Option #1

Add value to your tax prep services by bundling additional benefits for every client you help.

Don't just prepare someone's tax return. Provide tax planning advice, investment strategies, insurance options, real estate counsel or any host of extra services (money related is best) to set yourself apart and make your tax professional services extremely valuable for your clients.

Oh, and by the way. You'll be able to charge more, too. Your competition's instincts will be wrong. They will try and offer the same tax services as always, and cut their fees to try and save clients from leaving. The exact opposite strategy is best. Offer premium services for a premium price. You will work less, with fewer clients, but make more net profit.

Option #2

Begin offering additional services to your clients (who already trust your recommendations) and add new revenue streams to your tax practice.

This is the perfect time to move forward on a strategy that will birth a new business within your tax business. If your tax preparation income will be slowly but surely eroding away, today is the day to begin replacing this revenue.

There is a plethora of services you can begin selling to your existing tax clients. One of the easiest and most lucrative money-making services is buying and selling Tax Liens and Tax Deeds. Over the last 20 years, I've seen just about every well-matched-for-the-tax-industry business opportunity known to man. There's a specific system designed for tax business owners I endorse and recommend to my Members. If you want more info, email my office and we'll forward you the details about this extra revenue generating opportunity. **chauncey@taxmarketing.com**

Like I said, I believe your tax business needs to move forward on BOTH options. It's not enough to just go to IRS Tax Forum Seminars and complain to the powers that be. (Actually, this kind of mindset can be detrimental to your practice.)

Take personal responsibility for your tax business and begin taking steps forward on your journey to reshape the services you offer and position yourself to experience new income streams like you've never seen before.

The "49 Shortcut Strategies" in this book are a blueprint for you to make as much money as you can in the fastest way possible.

So tax pros ask me, "Why would I spend the money on acquiring new tax prep clients for tax season when these services are becoming more and more commoditized?"

The answer is simple.

You want to add as many NEW tax clients as you can, as quickly as you can, to build trust and relationship with them ASAP.

And when the Artificial Intelligence gets more and more mainstream and your tax prep fees go sideways, you'll have several other services to offer them which will generate extra revenue for you and your family as a result.

Bottom Line:
Read these "49 Shortcut Strategies to Make More Money Now" (while you still can)

Then implement.

If you don't execute and DO something to help your tax business, then this Crash Course Book of marketing advice will be just words on a page ….

I look forward to hearing your success story!

Chauncey's Epiphany That Built a Million Dollar Tax Business

Back in 1990, I just wanted to be able to make enough money to cover my house payment. I had just been laid off from a construction company that sold windows, doors and hardware to builders. After a series of conversations, I told my dad I thought I could expand his tax practice selling bookkeeping and payroll services. But secretly, I wanted the freedom to set my own schedule and have a chance to create wealth on someone else's dime.

The thing is I was only making one sale at a time. I'd drop in cold to an unsuspecting small business and inquire about their need for tax help. Cold calling over and over, one business at a time, was slow, and I was not able to grow my dad's tax practice fast enough to pay my commissions to live on. That meant once I covered my house payment for the month, there was hardly any money left for me to live on. I was scraping by, slowly expanding my dad's tax business and doing my best to "be free" and try to create wealth.

To make things worse, I felt terrible because I was working really hard, but had very little to show for my efforts. I felt even worse about the situation because I was getting a $200 per week draw on my commissions, which translated into only making between $2.00 and $2.50 per hour. Since my younger brother was earning $10.00 per hour as a bookkeeper, it was a little awkward on payday. Secretly, I felt like I was spinning my wheels, dragging down my dad's tax business.

A new problem surfaced during tax season. Now that all my dad's tax filing clients would be coming into the office soon, I had to switch my responsibilities from door-to-door tax service salesperson to marketer of our tax services during the filing season. This suddenly meant I was working even more hours for less money because I didn't have a chance to make commissions on my regular sales calls to small business accounts in the area. That meant I was stuck working 12 to 14 hour days, 6 days per week, and getting paid less than teenagers would working their first job.

Then, as if by chance, something amazing happened...

That's when I read a Dan Kennedy book about direct response marketing showing me how to leverage the power of words in print to do the selling for me! And not just one-at-a-time salesmanship like I had been doing. Dan's eye-opening advice was to place targeted ads directed to specific groups, so many people could respond to our tax business' marketing message at the same time. This helped us grow much faster and more efficiently.

I quickly gained clarity on how to write an attention-grabbing headline and make an irresistible offer, setting our tax business apart from our competition. This new promotional revelation allowed me to confidently invest money on media that matched our target market and turned a profit almost every time we promoted our tax business.

I also learned that not just anyone should answer the phone in your tax office because getting the phone call is only half the battle. Once an interested prospect calls your office, looking to give your tax business money to help them file their taxes with the IRS, only allow a trained sales person to answer the phone. If you allow a non-trained staff member to answer the phone, you might as well go down to the bank and get yourself a stack of $100 bills. Then come back to your office, walk into the bathroom and flush this cash money right down the toilet.

Because of more effective advertising and better stewardship of these inquiries coming into our tax business, I parlayed these increased revenue streams and invested even more in direct response marketing systems and modeled our tax biz ads after additional proven winners.

After I did that, we started getting overwhelmed with new clients calling our tax office and walking in off the street.

Suddenly, we had to expand the space in our office, add new computers and hire more employees to handle the flood of new tax clients.

That's when I realized that the secret to exponential growth was NOT cold calling new clients and offering our services to them one at a time. The breakthrough came when we leveraged a compelling message, focused on what our target clients wanted, and did so with marketing campaigns and advertising that sold many people at once. These tax business ads had to make our tax office's phone ring. After that, we let our trained phone person get them in the door to do business with us and not our competition.

After experiencing a tremendous success that first tax season, my plan was to start looking for new markets to open additional tax offices. I'm a builder. So, when we had a system working well in one location, naturally I wanted to replicate our success in other locations.

That's when I started driving to nearby cities before tax season ended to see what the brand name competition was up to. I was amazed how "behind" these supposed leaders were. How were these national tax franchises doing such a poor job, but still making money in their city? Watching what these competitors were doing as they ran their tax business gave me confidence we could expand into their area and take market share from them.

But we didn't stop there. We then began thinking strategically about what kind of managers to hire and how we would oversee these new offices to ensure quality control.
After that, we found 3 new tax office locations, signed leases, hired staff, bought equipment and of course, prepared a marketing plan.

But there was still a problem...

Each new location had new employees we had to trust to do an excellent job. Internally we gave them training manuals and how-to procedures. But once we left their office, we had to hope they were implementing everything the proper way. My marketing campaigns kept them busy. Getting the phone to ring off the hook was not the issue. Our problems came from the customer service side. These new employees were not going the extra mile (like an owner would do), so once we brought in a new client, too many didn't return the following tax season.

We grew so frustrated with the lack of quality service when an owner was not around, that we decided to create an online "big brother" software that could watch in real time what our employees were doing. We called it "The Automated Tax Manager."

[Note: If you're interested in the 2.0 version of the Auto Tax Manager software, email our office and we'll forward you the details. **chauncey@taxmarketing.com**]

We thought if we could create a system that linked accountability with our most important high profit margin services, we could schedule weekly promotions to drive new clients into our office and feel good about how these taxpayers would be taken care of. The marketing dollars were worth spending, but only if a higher percentage of first-time clients came back the second tax season.

By improving the quality of people we hired, tracking and measuring the most important matrixes in our office, we were able to blend Management and Marketing together to ensure maximum profits moving forward.

Now, for the last two decades, not just our tax business, but thousands of other tax pros have used our marketing, management and sales tools to grow their tax business effectively.

Today, our system is so refined, we can DOUBLE a tax business owner's profit in less than 100 days.

Here's what we were able to achieve:

In less than 10 years, we built a $4.3 million dollar per year tax business with 24 locations, 400 employees and over 27,000 new tax clients, all from my tax business marketing campaigns.

After creating this system, I was not only able to have the freedom to make my own schedule like I always wanted … but even better, I built significant wealth for our family. I also stopped working long hours and worrying about where the next income stream will come from.

Now I enjoy helping other tax pros glean from my tax business' growth experience.

Introduction:
Tax Marketing CRASH COURSE

Before getting started with the Tax Biz Success Crash Course, I want you to stop right now and take a deep breath.

My business was just like yours at one point, and we all know that feeling of pressure—heck, even envy—as we look at somebody else's success. And it's not a good feeling. So stop reading and spend some time in GRATITUDE for where you are right now. You'll find that you'll be able to go through this material with a much lighter heart after you take that time.

You back now? Good.

There's a lot of stuff here in my Crash Course, so I don't want you to feel overwhelmed. It's important that you keep your mind AND your heart on top of your game, and NOT let the demons of doubt and discouragement come at you as you embark on this journey with me. This Crash Course is going to be just what the doctor ordered, in terms of getting your tax business on an entirely new footing.

You may be feeling pressure and needing to have a "good" tax season this year, or you might be financially burdened with some debt you've been trying to get off your back for a while.

Or, maybe you already have a massively successful high-volume tax or accounting practice, but it has "leveled off" now and you feel like you (and your tax business) have hit a wall. It happens to the best of us. You need a breakthrough!

Well, if you fall into any of these categories, you are not alone. Even if you are just a regular tax business owner that's not financially strapped, but would like to have a "better-than-average" tax business just to put a few extra bucks in your pocket at the end of tax season, you've come to the right place.

You see, in this Tax Biz Success Crash Course you'll find the answers you're looking for no matter what situation you are in now … or where you want to go in the future. But before I take you down this road, I want to expand on some of the basic problems tax business owners are facing when they get their hands on our Crash Course material.

First of all, some of you will bring a certain level of fear. Fears like …

Can I actually do this? Of course you can. Did you know just by seeking me out and taking the time to read my tax business success material, you are ALREADY way ahead of 80% of all the other tax business owners in this country—**the TOP 20%**. You are already DOING what most everyone else in the tax industry is NOT and will NEVER do. You are seeking help from an expert who has been where you want to go.

Will I understand it? You better believe it! How do I know? It doesn't take a genius to follow my step by step action plan, learning from my mistakes ahead of time. If I don't speak plainly and clearly enough for you, just let me know, by emailing our Real Tax Business Success office at chauncey@taxmarketing.com.

What if I fail? If there is one thing that I have learned as I have watched the successful growth of tax businesses to the Million Dollar Level you FAIL your way into it! Ask any other top successful business owner in any other industry and they'll tell you the same thing. "Failing" is no big deal. I don't even look at a mistake as a failure; I see it as a RESULT. You get good results and bad results. You learn, and go on. (Fortunately for you, I've gotten enough "bad results" that your path to success will be MUCH easier than mine ever was!)

Your Tax Business Will NOT Change For The Better ... Unless YOU Decide To Change For The Better!

The biggest mistake you could ever make is to read through this Crash Course and NOT do anything with it! To get results, you have to DO something! We've got a step-by-step system for you to follow outlined in great detail in this book and it is PROVEN to be very effective, but ONLY if you use the material.

If you're ready to make some changes in how you run your tax business, then you've come to the right place. We're in the business of first helping tax business owners "see" their problems and then showing them the best ways to fix 'em!

Ready ... Set ... GO!

There's a lot of material in this Crash Course and a lot of good ideas to implement that will make you money. But don't be overwhelmed. As you read over the success secrets, you'll find some ideas that really apply to your situation, yet others that seem to be good, but you might not be ready for them yet.

That's OK. You see, my advice is to mark the steps you feel your tax business will need and use the most so you can go back to them later to review. This process was designed so you could read and re-read the material—but also get it in the right order, at the right time. There is so much information here, you actually can't do it all in one tax season!
Just review it bit by bit and you'll have plenty to do for this tax season.

Pick 5 or 10 strategies from the Crash Course that have the highest priority for you and your tax business. Then you will have a better chance of implementing your most productive ideas first.

I'm looking forward to working with you as you grow your tax business. Please fill me in on YOUR success story as it unfolds!

Strategy #2

The Most Important Reality You Must Accept

The mental shift from "doer of the task" (preparing tax returns) to "promoter of your business" (marketing tax services) is vital if you plan on growing your tax business to the Million Dollar Level. I would say over 99 percent of the tax business owners in America do not make this mental jump from "I do taxes for a living" to "I market my tax business for a living."

Now don't think I'm being picky here. This is important to get straight NOW, right up front.

Most tax business owners think "tax preparation" is the most important part of the business. That is simply not the case.

The tax business "doer" sees the task of preparing returns as their primary role. The tax business "promoter" sees acquiring clients, retaining them, and maximizing their total client value as their primary role. Tax preparation is seen as just another task in the office.

I hope you can see the difference. If you are hearing this concept for the first time, let it sink in and think about it for a second. If you don't have clients coming through your door, you could be the best tax practitioner in the world, but you're still going to starve.

The most important part of your business is "making the sale!" And the way you get someone in front of you to sell your tax services to is MARKETING.

Getting people to call your office saying, "I want to do business with you," and then to show up at your door wanting to give you money in return for a particular tax service **IS THE MOST IMPORTANT THING YOU NEED TO MASTER.**

This concept has to make sense to you or you will have a hard time making LARGE sums of money in the tax business.

For now, make sure you do this: AS YOU GO THROUGH THIS CRASH COURSE, **THINK OF WAYS YOU CAN MOVE FROM "DOER" TO "MARKETER"** IN ORDER TO INCREASE YOUR TAX BUSINESS AND MAKE IT MORE PROFITABLE FOR YOU DOWN THE ROAD!

And don't "box yourself in," saying, "But I'm not good at sales or marketing!"

You can't say that anymore now that you've gotten your hands on this Crash Course. Just by reading my Crash Course Book, you're light years ahead of almost all the other tax business owners in this country!

I know you don't want to be a "worker bee" (or a slave to your business) the rest of your life. It's time to change that mindset of yours, starting today.

In fact, here's one way you can do that:

Use the DOMINANT THOUGHT to accelerate the success of your goals!

I am NOT talking about some mystical "Law of Attraction." What I AM talking about is changing your mindset as a FIRST STEP to action. Simply by "thinking" something, doesn't mean you'll get it—but it DOES mean that your actions will slowly, but surely, begin to align themselves more with higher goals.

Here's an example:

If your dominant thought is, "I'm going to grow my tax business to the million dollar level, it's going to take me a certain number of years do to it, and I'm willing to do what it takes," and if you are constantly thinking about new ways to grow your tax business and find new clients, your chances of success GREATLY increase!

If that IS the dominant thought in your head, your subconscious is automatically going to help you get to where you want to go. It's one of these personal success principles that is true. I don't know how, but this subconscious stuff works. I can tell you that if this is what you're thinking about, you are naturally going to gravitate towards making it happen.

If your mind wanders during the day and but your dominant thought is what you're thinking about -- it will help you get to where you want to go faster.

Do not underestimate what I just said. This one little secret could make the difference between an average tax business and an extremely profitable tax business.

(Just make sure you choose your "dominant thought" carefully.)

Choice, Fear and Consequences

These first few steps may seem "dumb" to you. You may not want to think about or address these significant "mental blocks" to your success. But, in my experience—these are the **foundations** to Million Dollar Thinking. Chances are, a big reason you haven't hit that level (yet), is because of your thinking ... and because of your choices.

The choices you make NOW have the greatest impact in your life LATER.

I personally don't believe that there are any victims in life -- there are only "volunteers who choose to feel victimized."

We choose to "get a bad deal" on a purchase of office equipment if we don't do our homework ahead of time before the sale is made. We choose to put up with the "mean" irate client that yells at us in the lobby of our office. We even choose to have employees steal from us because we were too lazy to set up some kind of accountability system which "checks" for possible theft each day.

You see, we make good and bad choices every day. Sometimes we even let "life" choose for us by not making a decision at all!

One major example everyone in the tax business can relate to ...

It's April 30th, and you have fresh in your mind all the things you want to do to improve your tax business for next year. You even have them written down this year. Then eight months go by, and it's

January 1st again. Well, what happened?

You chose not to DO almost everything on your "to do" list that you were committed to do last April and May. That's okay, though, you think. Business is not so bad. You'll lose a few clients, and you'll pick up some more to replace them.
Do me a favor.

Now that you've started this Crash Course, I want you to CHOOSE to actually use it! And I don't mean right before next tax season, I mean NOW!

I don't care how good your tax business is right now, you can ALWAYS get a little bit better! If you just do a few little things each year, you'll be surprised how much of a difference it will make in your overall profitability.

I know from personal experience. The years I chose to DO what I planned to do are the years our tax business ran the smoothest and made the most profit. Yes, I know about making choices. I've made plenty of good ones and bad ones. All I'm asking you to do is choose a direction and actually go for it.

Don't do "nothing" and let life choose for you!

And another thing...

Self image and FEAR affect everything from your goals to how you grow your tax business!

If you have in your mind that you are a certain type of tax business owner that can't change, or that you are a "200 or 300 client" operation, and that's all the clients you feel you can handle, well -- YOU'RE RIGHT!

Until you change your thinking and your self-image, you will have a hard time doubling or tripling your business and keeping it at those profit levels for any extended length of time.

Why? Because none of us can outperform our own self-image for any extended length of time!

I can teach you how to get 1,000 new clients over the next three tax seasons, but if you don't think you can handle the growth of new business, or you don't know how you will oversee the added employees, then guess what?

You won't do what it takes to get there because it doesn't match up with the image you have of yourself.

Did you know your "FEAR" of the unknown will also stunt your tax business's growth? Fear is NOT a bad thing. It can be healthy at times. But if fear paralyzes you from taking action, then let me fill you in on what fear really stands for.

FEAR = False Evidence Appearing Real

That's right! 99% of what you fear never comes to pass, but the "fearsome" information in your head makes it seem real!

You see, I'm going to ask you to do a lot of different things in this course that you probably have never done before. If you are paralyzed by fear, then you will NOT benefit from our Crash Course. Why? Because you'll be too scared to DO anything I suggest.

Look, everyone has fear. We are all human. It's how you DEAL with fear that sets apart the successful people of the world. They actually fail MORE than anyone else because they are not afraid of it!

When a successful person tries something and it doesn't work out, that's fine. It's called a result. You have good results and bad results. Successful people don't see a bad result as negative. It's just new information that can be used to get better results in the future!

Remember: How a person handles failure (usually perceived through a poor self-image or fear of the unknown) determines how much success he or she can have.

Strategy #4

Small Business Marketing Success Means Starting At The Right Place!

Here's a secret that the VAST majority of tax professionals get WRONG. In fact, this is true of most every struggling small business on the block.

Selecting the "right or wrong" target market can be THE factor that determines success or failure!

Marketing means: Market first, message second, and media third, in that order. (And the order is important.)

The market is critical. It's the number one concern. If you don't get it right, the rest of your promotion won't matter. (You might as well save your money and go home.) You see, if you don't target the right market, even if your advertising message is outstanding and the media you choose is the most cost effective in the world, you'll still lose money.

(If they don't want what you got, it just doesn't matter what you tell them, how often you tell them or even how you tell them.)

If the BEST tax office in your region offers the BEST marketing message of anyone else around, but targets the wrong market, they will not do that well.

On the other hand, a VERY AVERAGE tax office with a VERY AVERAGE marketing message can find and target a well-selected market that is hungry for their services, and this tax business will be far more profitable than the first. (All because the market they were keying on WANTED what they were offering.)

So how do you find a "hungry crowd" that WANTS what tax services you are offering?

Let me tell you a story first.

Gary Halbert, a world renowned marketing expert, once coined a marketing term about the importance of the "market." He'd explain it something like this in his seminars:

"If I offered to set you up in a fast-food business like a hamburger joint and you could have one special advantage, what would it be? A clown, special sauce, great hamburgers, or a big ad budget?"

Well, Gary Halbert's answer was he would take a "starving crowd" over any other advantage you could give him. So basically he's saying that it is more important to have a group of people that are hungry to buy what you have than to have a good ad or a lot of money to spend on marketing.

Translation to those of us in the tax business: It is more important to find a "starving crowd" that's desperately looking for tax services than it is to have the best ads in town or the most money to spend on marketing.

Now notice *I didn't say,* "A starving crowd desperate to use the particular kind of tax services you offer in your business."

Remember my question: "How do you find a hungry crowd that WANTS what tax services you are offering?" That is a good next question to ask, but the end, "you are offering" is the problem.

You see, you don't go looking for a "starving market" that wants the kind of tax services you specifically offer (i.e. high-priced CPA services). Believe me, it's nice when the starving crowd in your town MATCHES up with what you already offer in your tax business. But other times it doesn't work out that way.

Tax marketing in its "purest" form means finding a "hungry group" of people and selling them the kind of tax services **they want!**

Let me give you a common example of what I mean.

An owner of a simple 1040 tax prep business asks me, "What's the best way to market my business?" Now I can tell him a bunch of stuff to do to get more clients, but the REAL answer is, "I wouldn't know until I found out HOW I CAN REACH the groups of people in YOUR TOWN that are the hungriest for various kinds of tax service."

This particular tax professional might want to set up a "retail, strip mall tax shop" so he doesn't have to do much preparation himself. But in his area, there are six other tax offices targeting the same group of taxpayers. Now all those tax businesses are probably doing a good job so that target market group is saturated with very little growth in sight.

On the other hand, John Smith CPA is the only game in town offering a high-end service to wealthy clientele. All the other mom n' pops in the area aren't doing a very good job competing with him, and there is an abundance of affluent clients just sitting there waiting to be taken. What should that tax professional do?

Some decide NOT to target the "starving crowd" and just do the same ol' thing they've always done. They will have some success because they will have learned to promote themselves better. Other CPAs will see that the group of clients they've been targeting in their town has gone flat. At the same time, they'll notice another possible market with some growth opportunity and decide to give it a try. It may be a "starving group" interested in their particular services or it may not.

The point is the SMART tax business owner focuses on the MARKET that's most responsive to ads and offers what the HUNGRY taxpayer wants!

His marketing job is made much easier, and the profits deposited in his bank account will come much faster.

Now I hope you can see why a "starving crowd" and finding the RIGHT MARKET is so important! We'll talk more about how to find these kinds of target groups through the rest of the lessons. But for now, you just need to know the market is the number one priority when growing your tax business.

Strategy #5

Avoid BIG Mistakes in Identifying
Target Markets

This might be a startler for you...

Target ONLY small markets!

Yes, I said, "Target only small markets!" You don't normally hear this coming from people talking about advertising. You mostly hear people say stuff like, "If I place this ad, it'll hit fifty thousand people," or "I can place this ad and it gets to everyone in the surrounding three counties."

But the truth is, this is NOT the way savvy marketers operate. If you are a small tax business owner you don't necessarily want to hit a hundred thousand people with your marketing message on some TV ad. The bigger the blanket or the more people you can reach at one time is not always the objective. It gets extremely expensive, and you end up wasting more money than you care to admit advertising this way. Successful marketers understand this and decide to at least start out a different way.

If EVERYONE is your client then, realistically, NO ONE is your client!

As a small business owner you need to spend your time finding small markets to target (i.e. small groups of people.) If you can find them, they will be much less expensive to attract, and you'll cut down on a tremendous amount of advertising waste.

Your target markets should be small enough for the marketing resources you commit to have a huge impact. What you don't want to do is waste your marketing dollars by spitting into the Atlantic Ocean.

When you promote your tax business, you want to be THE big fish in a small pond!

Let me explain what I mean in more detail.

Going back to tax business owners being too broad with their marketing and wanting to send their message out all over the place and hope something sticks…That just is NOT what you want to do! You want to select a small market so you can become a dominant player in that small niche. The big fish will win out more times than not!

Here's an example:
You happen to have a contact at a factory with 3,000 workers. You have an "in" with some managers, and they can get your promotional fliers up in all the break rooms. They also can get your promotional coupon in the company's W-2 envelopes they're handing out in January. You promote a special Saturday morning tax seminar in early to mid January for employees on what to do with their company retirement plan.

Do you get the point? You are dominating the small market of that factory. If an employee is going to pay a tax practitioner this year to help them with their taxes, you will have a greater opportunity to get this business than some other tax practice. There will be others who may be advertising, and their message will get out to those people, but you're the dominant player (in their minds) because you've specifically targeted "their world" and the group they hang out with.

Now do you only target that one market for your whole tax season? Absolutely not. **You want to pick two, three, five, ten or however many small markets you can realistically keep track of.** They either will fit the description of someone who already wants the tax services you're offering, or you'll see you need to offer a new kind of tax service in order to give them what they WANT.

Another example of being a big fish in a small pond could be the neighborhoods right around your office. (You always want to start your promoting in your own backyard.) You can do the same thing by advertising or sponsoring in the neighborhood newsletter during tax season. Have high school kids drop off door hangers on all the doors, offering some kind of Saturday afternoon, "take a break from your yard work and come see how not to pay any taxes" seminar. Or even set up a party around the holidays in a nice house in the neighborhood and offer a "FREE tax tips for the new year" get together.

Look, there are hundreds of "small markets" where you can be a "big fish in a small pond" in and around your town.

How about the local organizations you currently belong to? OR do you have close friends you can use as contacts to get you "in" the organizations THEY are involved in?

What about your church? I've got a client who has built a large tax practice by doing nothing more than promoting himself to individual churches, one at a time. Over the past few years I think he has "niche marketed" to over 100 different churches in and around his area.

I bet the parents at your kids' schools pay taxes. There's nothing wrong with being the "tax specialist" at their schools.
OK, you get the idea. Let's get even more specific.

There's riches in niches.

"Discriminating" is a GOOD word when you are marketing. (I'm referring to CHOOSING here!) When you discriminate you are saying you do NOT want to talk to a certain kind of person or group of people—with your marketing dollars!

Getting specific and selecting a "narrowed down" group is good marketing because the more "laser-beamed" and focused you can get, the better your market-to-message match will be.

If you know who that person is and what that person wants, you'll be able to discriminate more effectively and vastly increase your response rates for your target group.

If you really want to dominate a small market, you'll find a "niche group" of people you have a natural AFFINITY with.

Like I've already said, it's very good to target small markets and be the big fish in a small pond. But your marketing job becomes infinitely easier when you have an **affinity** with your targeted "niche" market.

You don't PERSONALLY have to have a tight affinity with a group (even though it's better if you do). Your association may be a little distant, but you can still make it work.

If you use the example of your church, your children's school, or some other association you're involved with, when you write the ad, you want to make your sales copy scream, "Hey, I'm one of you! Let me tell you how I can help you better than those other tax professionals."

Now that you have them on YOUR side, the marketing process becomes easier.

Here's an example of not having an *exact* affinity with a market, but it's good enough:

Maybe your spouse works in the medical profession, and he or she had contacts in the hospital. You can write a sales letter that goes out to everybody in the hospital describing how you know about their frustration, and you understand their pain in figuring out the new tax laws in the medical profession. You can do all this because you hear about it every day from your spouse.

Showing empathy toward your target market and being able to "tie your story" as close to where they live, eat, and breathe will dramatically increase your sales numbers!

Bill Clinton: A smart marketer. "I feel your pain" sounded stupid to many of us at the time. But it won over the "target groups" of voters he was talking to. Ol' Bill used AFFINITY marketing to get elected twice! Showing empathy to the voters will get you some votes.

Apply the same principle to your tax business. The same is true when you're marketing to a targeted group that you're at least trying to have an affinity with. If you can talk about how much pain you know they are in from working in their industry, and if you can empathize with how their tax situation is constantly changing and how it's so hard to deal with, you'll have a very RESPONSIVE market on your hands!

Then you go on to say, "Hey, that's why I specialize in this kind of work. Tax preparation for people like you who need help from a tax professional like me. I KNOW your situation and the tax implications for it. I specialize in that kind of work, and I give special discounts for people in this industry." (And I give free this, and complimentary that, ONLY for people in "our" group, etc.)

You are talking to them. You have an affinity with them! You understand their pain and frustration. People love doing business with people they have a bond with.

Whether you agree people should or shouldn't do business like this is not the point. The point is, people are going to give their money to other people for services rendered (i.e. taxes), so it might as well be YOU getting some of it.

It's good to be a specialist (or look like one).

Do you ever get referred to a specialist from a "general practitioner" doctor? Usually it takes a LOT longer to see a specialist than a GP.

And being a specialist or perceived as a specialist can turn an ordinary tax business into an EXTRAORDINARY tax business just by changing the "positioning" of your marketing a little. Higher prices can be charged, higher margins will be enjoyed, and being a specialist will help give you the "competitive differentiation" you'll need to make the sales! (The "big fish in a small pond" approach works even better when you say you specialize.)

When you target small markets, you'll be promoting offers to groups like doctors or lawyers or any other kind of specific profession. You'll be promoting to certain apartment complexes within a three-mile radius because they are "so close to our tax office, we're giving out special deals." (You could have five or six housing complexes you specialize in because they are so close to you.)

Or going back to the church example. You could promote yourself to the thirty churches in your city as the "tax professional specializing in helping people in our local church congregations" within a twenty mile radius of your office.

Again, all of these examples are just breaking down larger markets into smaller markets to help specific niche groups feel like you are talking specifically to them. This will always help you match your message with your market. The tighter the fit, the more success you'll have!

Remember, if targeting these smaller groups is the ONLY thing that causes your potential prospect to pick up the phone and at least give you a call, that's great! That's the only job of your advertising anyway -- to get you the phone call.

Keep thinking of ways you as a tax professional can POSITION yourself as a specialist to multiple niche markets in your area. Each tax business owner is different. Take whatever advantages you have and use them!

Working On What 99% Of Tax Professionals Royally Screw Up—The Message

First of all, if you scan the yellow pages (or Google) in your category, I'll make a bet with you: 90% of the ads -- actually probably ALL of them -- look very similar. They all offer the same services, with the same features.

What makes your tax business any different?

Well, here's a good place to start…

Giving taxpayers what they WANT is the place to start when developing a marketing message!

How do you make YOUR message stop your target market dead in their tracks? The only way to truly get their attention is to "give 'em what they want!"

Does your target market want a guarantee? If so, guaranteeing what? How many multiple guarantees backing up your tax services are they interested in? Sure, they may want a guarantee of accuracy, but many tax business owners do that. How will yours be different?

But don't stop there. Do your clients want a bigger waiting room or is "drop off" service a better option? Do your clients want your location to be closer to where they live or work? What about all their friends, neighbors and business associates that live and work in the same area?

What about the kind of employee you have representing you in your tax office? Does your target client want an experienced tax practitioner or just someone who takes one-on-one time with them and makes them feel important?

I can go on and on. **The point is, your marketing message must be centered around giving your target market everything they REALLY want, not what YOU THINK they want** and definitely not what you are just going to give them because "that's what other tax businesses do."

And as you can see, your message is NOT confined to just "what" kind of tax services you offer. Marketing deals with everything from how you say your guarantee to who is doing the selling to when you're actually going to follow up with your prospect (or existing client)!

So the big question is, "How do I find out what my target client wants?"

And the million dollar answer is ASK 'EM! (And continue to ask them more and more each tax season.)

Many tax business owners have hundreds and hundreds of client records sitting in their filing cabinets. These clients came into the tax office during previous tax seasons and the tax business knows nothing more about them than the information on their tax return.

Now, looking at someone's tax return can tell you a lot about them. But do you know a better way to find out more about them? Look at the phone number in the file and call them and ask them a few questions about what they would really want in the coming tax season. You will be amazed what you find.

If you're too lazy to make forty or fifty calls to get a sampling from your database of what your clients really want, then create four or five questions and put them on a one-page survey sheet.

You can: get feedback from your clients about what they want while they are in your office having their taxes prepared this year. You don't get better information for promoting your business THIS year, but it's a start in the right direction for next tax season.

By starting to properly promote your tax business, you won't fight as many uphill battles as most tax businesses do. Your marketing becomes much easier and you'll make more money if you're giving taxpayers EVERYTHING THEY WANT IN A TAX BUSINESS!

Let's Talk About a USP...

A USP is a **Unique Selling Proposition** and without it—you're sunk.

What is a Unique Selling Proposition and how do I develop one for my tax business? Good question. Now let's find the answer by answering this next question:

<u>Why should your prospect choose you or your tax services versus any other option available to them?</u>

In other words, what are the reasons a certain group of people would choose you compared to going down the street to the other five tax businesses? What makes your tax business different and unique? Why are you better? What do YOU do that is so special?

If you do NOT have a good answer to these questions and you can't say it in a clear, concise manner, then you will have a real problem marketing your tax business effectively over the long haul!

Folks, this is where the rubber meets the road. This is where you lay it on the line. Your reputation, your money, your whole business hinges on a well developed USP!

It amazes me, as many times as I talk about this subject, how so many tax business owners DON'T have good answers to these questions! I'm telling you, spend a solid three or four days thinking through this one area of your business, developing a solid USP message to "hang your tax business on," and it could make the difference in six figures of profit in the next few tax seasons alone for some tax business owners.

Some tax business owners I talk to say, "Well, I offer the same tax services all the other accountants in town do. How can I be unique or different?" Or they will tell me, "Well, I offer quality service. It's the people in my office that make the difference."

Now how many times do you hear EVERY business say in their advertising, "Our people make the difference!"

I hear that so much I want to get sick!

Don't get me wrong, people DO make a difference in services business. But clients see that for themselves once they are ALREADY IN your office. We are talking about selling propositions that make you so unique that someone who has not used your services before would call or come by your office to inquire about your tax services.

Oh, and as far as "offering the same tax services as all the other accountants in town," that may or may not be true. But just for the sake of argument, let's say you DID offer the exact same tax services as everyone else.

I'd be willing to bet you **YOU COULD DESCRIBE YOUR SERVICES IN A UNIQUE WAY THAT WOULD DIFFERENTIATE YOU FROM YOUR COMPETITION.**

Example:

A) Acme Tax Service offers low prices and a fast turn-around service!

B) Acme Tax Service GUARANTEES The Lowest Tax Preparation Price Compared To Those "National Brand Name Companies," Plus We Offer Our Special And Unique Promise To You: Your Tax Return Prepared In 1 Day Or You Don't Pay! (*call for details)

Now don't you think example "B" might SELL your prospect into giving you at least a phone call? (I think so, too.) Example "A" could be offering the exact same tax services at the exact same price and getting 95% of the tax returns prepared in 1 Day, too. All example "B" has to do is make up a simple flier in their office, answer a few of the same questions over the phone, explain that 95% of the tax returns they prepare qualify for the 1 Day guarantee, and, instruct callers to please bring all their information down to the office and we'll find out ahead of time if their tax return qualifies.

So with the "B" tax business's two unique selling propositions, they will get MORE phone calls from their current advertising, which will result in MORE sales (and more income in their bank account).

Are you starting to see how important your USP message is to the overall profitability of your tax business?

You can have multiple USPs for multiple different target markets.

"Blue Collar" target market USPs:

- Fastest Tax Refunds Allowed By The IRS .... Guaranteed
- GUARANTEED Next Day Tax Preparation Services
- Our Promise: "The tax return will be correct or we pay the penalties and interest on our mistake!"

"White Collar" target market USPs:

- "Complete Peace Of Mind, IRS Protected" Accuracy Guarantee
- "No-Client-Waits" Executive Tax Service Guarantee
- "Special Procrastinator Discount Valid Until 6 p.m. April 14th"

If you have an answer to the USP question that is better than the other tax businesses in your town, you WILL get your share of phone calls this tax season!

And like I've said before (and I'll say it again), getting the phone call is THE goal of your advertising and marketing promotions.

How You Get A Target Client To *Take Action*

How do you do it?

Make "irresistible" offers to your target market!

Irresistible offers? Most tax business owners either don't know what an "offer" is, or they just don't use them in their advertising. And if they are using an offer in their promotions, they think saying, "Please call for a free consultation," is the most irresistible offer in the world. (You would not believe how many times "free consultation" comes across my desk when I do ad critiques for my Real Tax Business Success Members and personal consulting clients.)

** Quick Tip: If you have a "free consultation" you'd like to promote, that's fine. But spend some time and come up with a new "selling" title for your consultation. The public is TIRED of professional service businesses advertising with those same ol' two words. (Remember: USP)

What is an offer supposed to do? An offer should be either THE reason or one of the reasons the client "moves towards action" and contacts your tax service.

A good offer helps "close the sale!" Just the offer alone can make the difference between an average promotion and a big "money-making" hit!

So what do most ads in the tax business look like? They say, "We are Joe's Tax Service. Here's a $20 coupon. Use us this year for your tax needs." Or, they say, "XYZ Tax Service. We've been in business 25 years. Call us for your free consultation."

Now don't get me wrong, those are "offers," but if you spend some time thinking about it, you can develop some "irresistible offers" that will knock your clients' socks off!

You see, your competitors will continue to have weak, wimpy and "ordinary" offers like I've already described. (Borrrrring.) But you can promote BOLD, GUARANTEED, RISK-FREE "SELLING" offers that will blow your competition away and give you a series of unique selling propositions that set you apart from all the other tax businesses in your area.

The goal of your IRRESISTIBLE OFFER is to have your targeted client say in his mind (if not out loud), "I'd be a darn fool if I said 'NO' to this offer!"

If you have your targeted client thinking this way once they read, hear, or listen to your series of USPs or one outstanding irresistible offer, get ready for the stampede, because they will be coming!

What makes an irresistible offer so "irresistible?" When the client REALLY WANTS what you are offering. If the target market doesn't want it, your USP or irresistible offer is not going to go over very well.

Tax business owners underestimate what it takes to actually make a prospect get up off the couch, go to the phone, and call you (much less actually come down to your tax office and give you their money).

If you can get a person to pick up the phone right after reading your sales letter or seeing your ad on TV or whatever, the power of your offer is probably pretty good!

Let's talk about some examples.

My strategy for developing an irresistible offer comes from the "Ginsu Knife" technique.

You remember the ads: "This knife is so amazing and it only costs $19.95. But as an added bonus we will give you these extra knives. And to go with that, we'll throw this in for free. And if you call right now we'll include this other extra thing, but we can't offer it if you wait and call later. So that means you get these 21 things for only $19.95 ..."

Yes, it sounds "cheesy," but it works. And if you are interested in results you'll learn from that example and tailor your marketing message accordingly.

Here's what we do. (This example is from one of our old ads targeting the "blue collar" market.)

In an ad we'll offer:
- Fastest Tax Refunds Allowed By The IRS -- GUARANTEED!
- 1 Day (Sometimes SAME Day) Tax Preparation Service
- A "Complete Peace Of Mind" Accuracy Guarantee
- Open Year Round (with 30+ years in the tax business)
- $33 Off Coupon on any tax service (with deadline date)
- Added bonus: $25 worth of Free Gifts for each tax return prepared
- An additional "Special New Client Offer" limited to 1st 10 callers

Now if you were a "blue collar" taxpayer looking for a tax firm to help you with your taxes this year and you saw two different style ads -- one "Free Consultation" ad or an ad with the above USPs LISTED TOGETHER, MAKING AN IRRESISTIBLE OFFER -- which one do you think would at least get a phone call?
Don't you think the potential client might think, "I'd have to be crazy not to at least call these guys and see if they offer quality tax services?"

I rest my case.

Now you can do the same thing for a "white collar" market, for bookkeeping or payroll services -- anything you're offering out of your office.

Don't promote it as "wimpy" or "boring!" Use the power of an IRRESISTIBLE OFFER to set your tax business above the rest.

And like I always say ...

"ALL YOU HAVE TO DO IS BE A LITTLE BIT BETTER THAN OTHER TAX BUSINESS OWNERS IN YOUR AREA, AND YOU'LL GET DISPROPORTIONATELY MORE THAN YOUR FAIR SHARE OF TAX BUSINESS!"

In the land of the blind, the one-eyed man IS king.

Fundamental (And Most-Often-Missed) Copywriting Techniques For "Best Response" Tax Business Marketing (Part 1)

In the next few Lessons, we'll be going over what most Tax Professionals "miss" when they communicate with prospects, clients, and even staff. Implementing these often-overlooked secrets were fundamental to our tax business success.

You Must Get Specific.

If you want USPs that are extremely effective -- if you know what your clients want -- and you are trying to develop irresistible offers that will make the phone ring off the hook -- then no matter what you do, SAY IT USING MEANINGFUL SPECIFICS, not the same ol' vague generalities everyone else is using.

This is one of the easiest ways to stand out from the crowd because most ads in the tax industry I see talk in very "vague and general" language.

When tax business owners promote with generalities, their words and phrases actually have little meaning because they could be talking to anyone, seemingly about anything.

Here's a sampling of phrases I see in tax business owners' ads:

-reasonable rates

-guaranteed satisfaction
-prompt and quality service
OK. What would I do different? How about ...

- "Lowest Price Guarantee: We're cheaper than H & R Block, or we'll prepare FREE!"

(not that I would actually recommend this approach!)

-"You're satisfied with our tax service or we'll give you ALL your money back, plus a $50 bill for your time and trouble -- GUARANTEED!"

-"1 Day Tax Service and a guarantee the return is correct... or you don't pay a dime!"

Now there are three examples of how to beat the pants off your competition if they STILL insist on promoting vague and general phrases in their advertising.

When you are deciding on what kind of MEANINGFUL SPECIFICS are best for your business, remember these three techniques:

First, make sure you know what your MAIN competition is offering and promoting. Then, as you put your ads together, make sure your message clearly differentiates you from them AS A BETTER OPTION for your target market!

Second, BE GUTSY AND GIVE YOUR CLIENTS A WAY OF HOLDING YOU ACCOUNTABLE TO A HIGHER STANDARD OF SERVICE AND QUALITY! Guarantees with specific "timetables" usually scare off regular tax practitioners not interested in taking their tax business to the next level. Once you "lay it on the line" in your promotions, you WILL make it a priority with your staff to follow through with the HIGHER standard of quality and service.

And third, be bold. MAKE A BOLD PROMISE! Try something

like ...

"I Promise Your Complete Satisfaction With My Tax Service Or I'll Give You ALL Your Money Back, Plus A Clean, Crisp $50 Bill For Your Time And Trouble -- I GUARANTEE It!"

Believe me -- that as a headline, with your picture off to the side, of a sales letter will get some attention. You are making a SPECIFIC promise that is bold and gutsy. Your clients will like that!

Premiums and Bonuses Work VERY Well For Tax Businesses!

Giving people somethin' for nothin' will never go out of style. Everyone likes getting FREE stuff!

Even when someone sees an ad that says "free something" and the thought runs through their head, "Nothing is free" ... many times that person will STILL see what is being offered at no charge!

Even the biggest skeptic deep down wants (and hopes) to get something for nothing. That is why they keep reading the ad!

For a number of years Dominos Pizza ran a national ad campaign called, Somethin' For Nothin'! Their pitch: Buy our pizza, and we'll give you FREE drinks and an extra order of buffalo wings for nothin'!

(If you are about to order a pizza, and Dominos is offering a couple of extra "freebies" and the other pizza business in town isn't, wouldn't you at least call Dominos and see what the "whole deal" really is before committing to one company or the other?

Most people would. You see, Dominos Pizza is banking on the belief that they will get their share of phone calls because of this promotion. For a long time, it was their main Unique Selling Proposition.

Do you remember the USP that built the Dominos empire from one small pizza joint on a college campus to a billion-dollar, worldwide company? "Fresh, Hot Pizza Delivered In 30 Minutes Or Less -- GUARANTEED!" Talk about transforming an industry -- they set the standard for everyone else!

Back to this whole "something for nothing" promotional strategy:

Don't just think this only applies to a "lower end" client and that your "high end" clients would never go for a promotion like this. That couldn't be further from the truth.

I can't tell you how many times the "high end" clients of my father's personal bookkeeping & tax service would see our other commercial electronic filing and tax business advertising $10 off tax preparation fees, and it would get their attention.

Well, they see my dad's name on those ads and bring a little coupon in to get $10 off their $850 tax preparation fees. So he billed them $840 for that year's tax return. (No, I'm not kidding.)

Everyone likes to get a "deal," no matter how much money they have. The same is even MORE true when it comes to "rich folks" getting SOMETHING FOR NOTHING.

A few years ago the state lottery winner came from our home town. Three weeks went by without anyone claiming the winning ticket. Finally, an elderly woman showed up with the "lucky numbers," and she claimed her money. Why had she waited so long? Turns out she was a little embarrassed to let people know she was "playing lotto." She just happened to be one of the most wealthy individuals in the area. Her family's estimated net worth was in the hundreds of millions. So you see, even multi-millionaires like getting "something for nothing!"

So as a tax business owner, what can you offer in your promotions to take advantage of this "something for nothing" strategy?

Well, you can offer gifts and other "add-on" services that don't cost you anything . (i.e. FREE electronic filing and $25 worth of FREE gifts for each paid tax return).

Something else we offered in certain promotions was a FREE state return prepared if we do the federal ($35 value). It's hardly extra work for us to prepare a state return once we've completed the federal. (Push two extra buttons on the keyboard.) And to some people this was a better "value" than other free things we offered.

There's nothing wrong with giving your clients their choice of some free stuff, but just don't make it complicated. If doing a FREE state return hits your target market's "hot buttons" better than something else, DO IT!

Just make sure that whatever FREE promotion you do offer increases your overall volume at the same time.

Keep using your "something for nothing" promotions even when you get tired of seeing them. As long as your clients like them and your RESULTS equal increased overall profits, don't cut off that gravy train! (It'll probably never stop working.)

Fundamental (And Most-Often-Missed) Copywriting Techniques For "Best Response" Tax Business Marketing (Part 2)

It Really Does Matter What You Call Things!

A fact of life is: whatever you sell (in our case, tax services), you'll sell MORE if you add bonuses or premiums (that relate to your product or service) to the main offer.

We talked about the "Ginsu Knife" technique and the "something for nothing" strategy. But if what you are piling on as your added bonuses or premiums don't relate to what you're selling, or if these "free gifts" don't help advance the sales process in some way, you are wasting your time and probably losing some money in the process!

How do you know if the bonuses and premiums you want to offer will help stimulate sales and/or increase word of mouth referrals? **Well, ultimately you don't know until you actually "test" a few things first.**

What do you need to do before you start spending money on "tests" to increase your odds of success? Well, first remember that if the client doesn't care or doesn't want what you are offering as a premium or free gift, it doesn't matter what you call it, the promotional strategy will not work for the long term.

Also, make sure that, before you start naming or titling your bonus

for a premium, you can put it together yourself (or purchase)
each unit cheaply enough that your expense is minimal, but your
PERCEIVED VALUE IS HIGH!

Let me give you an example:

Buy a few booklets (or, better, make your own pamphlets) and use
them as bonuses for one of your target markets. Let's say you want to
offer a bonus to the "white collar, middle income" market to help sell
your tax services better.

You could advertise as a bonus, "FREE Investor's Handbook: *11
Secret Tips To Investing Without Risk That Save You Money On
Your Taxes At The Same Time!*"

If that is one of the services you could provide your clients and it is
a "hot button" for your target market, then the bonus WILL increase
the response to your ads! In some cases you'll find the actual "bonus"
you're offering for free is what the client wants more than the actual
service you may be offering.

But what if we just call the bonus, "FREE Investor's Handbook!"
Do you think the title will make a difference? You bet it will. (If you
don't believe me, "split test" it yourself. I'll bet you a dollar to a donut
the better "selling" title will win.)

If you can offer multiple "selling titled" premiums it's even better.
Using that same middle income target market I could offer the...

-FREE Investor's Handbook: *11 Secret Tips To Investing
Without Risk That Save You Money On Your Taxes At The
Same Time!*

-FREE REPORT: *Wealth Strategies Your "Other" Accountant
Never Told You About That Cost You Profit Every Day You
Don't Have This Report In Your Hands!*

-Plus a "MYSTERY GIFT" which automatically puts more
money in your home budget! (For new clients who call our

office and specifically ask for it by 2/28 ONLY!)

A tax business owner who tests this technique of using "selling titles" will make more sales. The tax business owner which tests multiple selling titles of their bonuses or premiums will do even better.

How you SAY things counts! And "Selling TITLES" will make the difference!

Just think about how many potential clients read your ads and are this close to calling you but just…don't. Multiple premiums with proper selling titles will get a good percentage of them off the fence and on the phone calling your office.

But you won't know how many "fencers" are out there until you start testing your titles and getting some of them in your doors.

But Can You GUARANTEE IT?

I always tell my clients in the higher level Coaching Groups, "If you can't make a strong and bold guarantee backing up your tax services, you need to get out of the tax business altogether!"

I really mean that, too. If you can't look a taxpayer in the eye and guarantee you'll take care of them with a specific predetermined promise, then why are you even showing up for work? What makes you different? What makes someone come to you for tax services? (Sound familiar from the USP section?) **One of the most common ways to offer an excellent USP is through a specific promise or guarantee made by the owner of the company.**

Important: USE A GUARANTEE AS A "SELLING OPPORTUNITY" -- NOT A PLACE TO STATE POLICY OR PROCEDURE. Instead, set your office up and train your employees to follow a system of policies and procedures to ensure you "back up" what you say you'll do in your guarantee!

And as a side note: The more SPECIFIC accountability you hold your guarantee to, the better your employees will have to perform to meet the client's expectations.

For the most part, most tax businesses don't state a written guarantee in their advertising. Usually tax business owners guarantee the tax returns they prepare for accuracy. If for some reason something is wrong with the tax return, they will fix it for free and/or pay any penalties and interest on that mistake.

The problem is not the guarantee. The problem is the owner not promoting it properly. (They're thinking more along the lines of actually having to "pay out" instead of what a bold guarantee would "bring in" with respect to new sales.)

PROMOTING A POWERFUL GUARANTEE WILL INCREASE YOUR OVERALL PROFIT EVEN IF YOU HAVE TO REFUND SOME MONEY!

Example:

Tax Business #1 has a basic guarantee. If the return is wrong, he'll fix it at no charge. He doesn't boldly guarantee the speed of his service. He prepared 200 tax returns this year. No increase from previous year.

Tax Business #2 develops a strong USP from a bold guarantee: *Tax Returns Prepared In 24 Hours GUARANTEED*. "We guarantee a one day turn around with the return being completely accurate, or you don't pay us a penny!"

(He knows his target market WANTS a fast turn around on their tax preparation services, so he promotes this bold, USP with "meaningful specifics" to his target clients.)

This tax business ended up "paying out" or preparing 20 tax returns for free standing by their guarantee. But the overall number of tax returns completed in his office this tax season was 450, up 250 returns from last year's total of 200.

Now what tax business would you rather be running, #1 or #2?

It's easy to see it makes more sense to pay out a few refunds (or not charge someone for their tax service) and get a bigger piece of the pie than to have no refunds (or no free tax returns) and receive a smaller piece of your city's tax preparation pie! Never stop thinking about your overall "big picture" profits and how a powerful guarantee can vastly improve your current situation!

PLEASE Do Not Be Boring!

This may be THE top reason tax business owners don't get a better response from their advertising. Most tax practitioners' ads are just flat out boring! (If you are guilty of this sin, confess it now and let's do something to change that tune forever!)

If 99% of all the accountants, tax preparers, bookkeepers and CPAs have boring ads…what do you think would happen if you got IN the 1% of the ads that "attract interest" and "hold the reader's attention?" You guessed it. You'd stick out like a fox in the hen house, eatin' up sales left and right!

One way to develop ATTENTION GETTING headlines and HOLD THE READER'S ATTENTION in your subheads and sales copy is to write your copy like it's a news story. You read the papers. You see the headlines in these news magazines. Same with online stories.

People will read your "attention getting" headline as if it were a regular story.

(Hint: This is the main reason why advertorials work so well in printed media. People think your ad is an actual story, so it gets read. Other ads that look like "ads" get passed over.)

If the headline interests them, they read on, and when they are finished, you've got a good chance at a sale. For those other tax practitioners going the "image" advertising route, their ads get thrown away with that day's garbage!

If you want to get down to the nitty gritty of it all, the heart and soul of advertising really is proclaiming news. Hopefully your advertising is proclaiming "good news" about how your service is better than the next guy, and at the same time it's interesting, not boring!

And if you don't have something NEWSWORTHY, you've got a message problem that has to be fixed! Don't be another one of those CPA firms or mom n' pop offices that advertises using the "dreaded" business card look (name, address, phone number, and "I prepare taxes, so come see me.") That's basically the ad.

If that's all you can say about your business, then you are NOT really advertising. That's NOT newsworthy! (Talk about flushing money down the toilet.)

Have a good reason to advertise. Make it newsworthy. You're a specialized tax practitioner that is helping a certain group of people, and these are the reasons why people are doing business with you. It's an "Unheard Of, Incredible, No-Risk Guarantee," or "FREE tax returns prepared for first time filers if we prepare your parent's tax return," etc.

You know you can come up with something newsworthy to proclaim to your town.

Just take some time a think about it. You'll be surprised what you can come up with that's NOT boring!

Fundamental (And Most-Often-Missed) Copywriting Techniques For "Best Response" Tax Business Marketing (Part 3)

Two Is Better Than One...

Now that you know about the importance guarantees are to growing your tax business, what's stopping you from having two? Two bold, gutsy guarantees will out sell one. Three out sells two.

I would analyze the three or four areas of your business your target client is the most concerned about -- speed, accuracy, no waiting, or not getting audited, just to name a few -- and offer "irresistible selling" guarantees to back them up! Remember, you're trying to get your potential client to say, "I'd have to be crazy NOT to give this tax practitioner a call!"

Important: **Keep as many "conditions" off your guarantees as possible.** One, they "water down" the salesmanship of the offer, and, two, you can get into trouble with unsatisfied clients!

For instance, look at this guarantee:

"I Promise Your Complete Satisfaction With My Tax Service, Or I'll Give You ALL Your Money Back, Plus A Clean, Crisp $50 Bill For Your Time And Trouble -- I GUARANTEE It!"

Now if you start putting CONDITIONS on "satisfaction," you will not only water down this bold guarantee, you'll get in a "nickel & dime" fight over the particulars of your guarantee with your client (and that's NOT where you want to be).

Yes, you are going to have a few clients come into your office and waste your time and rip you off for some tax knowledge. They will say, "I'm not happy with the amount of taxes you say I owe the IRS; I want to go to another accountant."

The next guy is going to tell them the same thing, but the problem is… with your guarantee, she can take her W-2s, 1099s, and whatever else with her and not pay you for the time you spent with her.

Don't worry about it. Remember the BIG PICTURE! This kind of guarantee could land you 100 new clients that you wouldn't have gotten if you didn't promote it. So what if you have five guys waste your time! You've made an extra 95 sales, which should translate into five figures of extra gross sales for your office. That's the number you should be focused on!

So let's keep talking about MORE guarantees and how the "multiple effect" increases your response. Why do multiples work so well? Mainly because you keep beating reasons into the client's head as to why you are the best option for them this tax season. And don't forget, the more guarantees you have, the more chances of hitting one of those HOT BUTTONS!

Here are some examples of guarantees you could use for different target markets:

- 24 Hour Tax Preparation Service -- GUARANTEED
- No-Client-Waits -- GUARANTEED
- Prepared Correctly Or You Don't Pay -- GUARANTEED
- No IRS Agent Will Ever Hassle You -- GUARANTEED

You'll be offering multiple guarantees and your competitors will offer none or maybe one weak guarantee. Taxpayers will have to make a choice … just make sure you have someone answering the phone that will do a good job making the appointment!

"Just Prove It To Me Baby!"

What will many of your potential prospects automatically think of when they see your advertising? What's one of the top reasons someone will not use your services? How come some people will remain stubbornly reluctant to "believe" any word you say?

The answers to these questions have to do with people's natural skepticism towards promotions, which arises when they see ANY ad. This is ESPECIALLY true in our fast paced, social media and online video news age.

How do you increase your odds when you're dealing with a skeptical public that may or may not believe any word you say? The answer lies in the PREPONDERANCE OF PROOF you add to all of your advertising!

What do I mean by "preponderance of proof?" It basically means showing your prospect beyond a shadow of a doubt you are who you say you are. That you can follow through like you say you can.

And the best way to "prove" to your client you mean what you say in your guarantee or in your promise to your clients IS TO HAVE SOMEONE ELSE SAY IT FOR YOU!

That's right! Strong testimonials, giving specific "testimony" to the benefits of your tax services.

Not: "Joe is a really nice guy and he did a good job preparing my tax return." Instead, get testimonials from your best clients that say, "Joe bent over backwards to make sure our tax return was completely correct. We came into his office Tuesday morning, and he took care of all the tax forms and filed our return electronically before five o'clock that same day!"

Do you see the difference between regular ol', "He's a really, really,

really good guy," versus stating specific details and benefits that the client remembers and enjoyed? Not only do the specifics sell better, the "believability" factor goes up, and you do a better job pitching your preponderance of proof case.

How do you get good testimonials? Ask for them! And if you want even more, interview your clients, write down what they say and then write out the testimonial for them. After you have written a paragraph or two, email your clients saying, "This is about what I heard you say over the phone, could you make any changes on this sheet of paper to make sure it is an accurate testimonial?"

(You do this because people will procrastinate and not write you a testimonial when they said they would. This is a good way to help them do it, by almost doing it for them!)

Now you'll have one more base covered to help increase your overall response rates in your promotional plan.

What Works For Best Buy Can Work For You, Too...

Why would you try to "reinvent the wheel" when you could use TESTED AND PROVEN MARKETING MESSAGES to increase the sales of your tax services?

This one may surprise you:

"I have never made the slightest effort to compose anything original."
Wolfgang Amadeus Mozart

And I bet you thought this guy sat up nights trying to be "creative or original" when he was composing new music?

Like most successful artists (and more importantly--successful business owners), you can take different ideas, formulas or services and combine them; then switch them around in a different order and PRESTO! Many "parts" of other successful projects rolled together as one make an another "original" message of its own.

How do I come up with successful ad headlines, unique ways to advertise for employees, or write a "selling formatted" letter? Simple. I look at other industries, see what is working and doing well for them and see if I can apply it to our tax business.

Don't get hung up on having to create an original marketing message. Hey, if saying "FREE Electronic Filing" helps increase the response of your headline, then use it! I see too many tax businesses trying to get "cute" with "original" headlines and the ad falls flat on its face.

As long as you are not breaking copyright laws, you are fine.

The whole point of going through this Crash Course is for you to take what we've learned over the years and mold and shape different parts of our success to fit your tax business so you do NOT have to reinvent the wheel promoting YOUR tax business!

Strategy #11

Fundamental (And Most-Often-Missed) Copywriting Techniques For "Best Response" Tax Business Marketing (Part 4)

Follow Proven Copywriting Patterns

This same principle of using "proven success" applies here but in a more specific way.

You see, there are many different sales formulas that have worked over the years in many different industries. I'll list some of the "classic" ones here:

- Problem - Agitate - Solve
- Attention - Interest - Desire - Action
- "I Predict"
- Shocking Facts
- GUARANTEE First

The sales formula many tax business owners use (with probably some success) is "Attention - Interest - Desire - Action." If your attention getting headline is a powerful one (with a strong USP), and your "offer" is IRRESISTIBLE with some good "take away" selling closes, you should get some solid results with a good mailing list.

Personally, my favorite sales formula to use is "Problem, Agitate the problem, then Solve it." Why? Well, it's easy to make this work since we are talking about taxes, and we have Uncle Sam on our side scaring the American public to death.

I can come up with a bunch of problems people have with our tax system (to grab attention) and tie it in with the target market. I can then agitate the heck out of the problem by talking about how evil the IRS is and "You better get your tax mess taken care of, or else." Then at the end, give the reader the solution they have been waiting for: our tax business. We will take all their problems away and provide this whole list of benefits.

You can apply this same sales formula to a new-homeowner letter, a Val-Pak coupon, a newspaper display ad (advertorial, of course), and even some neighborhood fliers!

Here's how to create a good new homeowner letter:

> Imagine a client that is somewhat frustrated, just moving to town after buying a new house. She is starting a new career and will have additional changes on her tax return besides the mortgage information. I know there is at least some underlying fear there so that's where I start with stating the problem: The tax code is always changing, new rules keep coming up, and she doesn't know if she can get it all straight. And she definitely doesn't want to take a chance of being audited by a nasty IRS agent!
>
> My headline would say, "Warning: New Homeowners! Filing Your Tax Return 'Wrong' This Year Could Be Hazardous To Your Pocketbook!"
>
> To agitate the problem my sales copy would say things like, "Uncle Sam will accept your filed tax return this year even if you are leaving off legal tax deductions that would keep more of your hard-earned money in your pocket!" And, " ... IRS audits? They can be costly, time consuming and even embarrassing!"
>
> So then, as the prospect seeks a solution, the copy reads, "Good News! My tax firm will not only prepare your tax return

and GUARANTEE its accuracy, but we'll help you keep the highest amount of money legally possible without having to worry about an IRS audit!"

You see, you're a tax professional. You do this for a living ... etc. (You get the idea.)

The main point here is THE SALES FORMULA.

DON'T JUST WRITE ANY OLD SALES LETTER OR PUT TOGETHER ANY OLD AD, USE A SALES FORMULA (ESPECIALLY THIS ONE) TO INCREASE SALES.

The Story's The Thing

Everyone has a story. I don't care who you are or where you come from, there is a story behind you and your business.

Why would I want to tell my story when I'm advertising, you ask? Of course, the reason is going to be INCREASED RESPONSE! Stories sell and you very rarely see them "promoted" in the tax industry.

What do I mean by "your story" and how long are we talking about? Depending on how much sales copy space you have to work with, the story you tell can be as much as a few pages in a sales letter to one sentence in a coupon flier on the street.

Your story could be about you and how you got started in the tax business. It could be, "I started working out of my home helping my neighbors with their taxes, and now it's 20 years later and I've got the largest tax firm in the downtown area servicing our town and the surrounding five counties."

You know YOUR story, so include it as you have the space in your ad copy.

People love stories. Growing up, we have been conditioned to pay attention to stories. You probably remember being read to sometime in your childhood. I think we all have our favorite stories we remember. Heck, even Jesus held people's attention by telling stories (parables) in the Bible.

If a strong USP headline can get your prospect's attention, then adding an interesting story to your sales copy will "keep" your reader IN your sales message better.

Adding your story to your marketing message is going to "kill many birds with one stone." You will make your sales copy more interesting (not committing the ultimate marketing sin of being boring.) You can increase your "believability factor" and reduce your prospect's natural skeptical nature with a story. And, finally, you can actually develop an additional USP if your story is good.

You'll totally distance yourself from your competition because they will just keep saying the same ol' stuff, but you'll be telling a story that sets you apart!

If adding stories to your marketing message didn't matter, I wouldn't tell you about it. But I'm here to say, telling your story EVERY time (adding one line if that's all the space you have), EVEN if you're talking to your existing clients, makes a difference.

A real simple way to do it, by the way, is with a regular monthly newsletter. Just not one of those boring "off-the-shelf" newsletters, but one that actually gives your clients and prospects a taste of your unique personality.

"Pre-Selling" Price and Positioning

In too many cases I see tax business owners let their clients dictate how they run their business. I guess they have bought into that old adage, "The client is always right."

Boy, that couldn't be farther from the truth when it comes to running a successful business in the "real" world! (Sorry, Tom Peters and all you other "academic" business book writers.)

You see, the only time you let your clients dictate your business is through sales.

If they WANT "this," and you are willing to give it to them, then great -- that's the way marketing is supposed to work. If they say, "I want you to give it to me faster," and if actual SALES can be attributed to how fast you give them what they want, and YOU are willing to do it this way, then great, make even more sales that way.

In order to run an even more efficient operation (especially during tax season) you have to SHAPE CLIENT EXPECTATIONS AHEAD OF TIME IN YOUR MARKETING MESSAGE.

If you advertise "Fast Tax Refunds from the IRS" for those that qualify, and on one particular day you happen to be understaffed, and the line in your office is increasing faster by the hour, how do you shape your clients' expectations in your marketing message?

By answering the phone with, "If you qualify for our Faster Tax Refund Services, please come into our office before 8 tonight.

After that we will not be able to take any more tax returns to file electronically because of our high volume of clients today."

Another way to shape your clients' expectations in your marketing message could be in a sales letter to one of your target markets. Some of your sales copy could read:

....

Are You Still Not Sure?

Well, I guess that's possible. You may have other questions or concerns I have not addressed yet. Maybe price or the cost of our tax services is an issue. It's a fair question. **So let me explain how we charge for the work that we provide for our clients.**

<u>If you are a person who usually looks for the "cheapest option" in town, let me just say right out of the gate</u>, **please do not contact our office.** We are NOT going to be the lowest price. You can go find other accountants, CPAs, or professional tax preparers in our area who will give you a "low-ball" price. Some are cheap, not offering much value. Other tax professionals quote you a low price now to get your business, and then sock it to you later on, once you've forked over all your tax related documents. We don't play that game. We also are NOT like some other bookkeepers here locally who will quote you a lower monthly rate for minimal work, but as that wise old saying goes, *"You truly do get what you pay for."*

Does that mean our accounting fees and other tax related services are priced too high? No, that is not the case. From what we know in our industry and from being active in the marketplace -- <u>our tax firm is somewhere in the middle as far as price goes</u>. **So when it comes to paying for professional tax services for your small business, you will NOT spend "an arm and a leg" working with us!**

But honestly, as a business owner, you should already know *VALUE means much more than PRICE any day of the week!* What you get from us, and how our services help you where you need it most, is MUCH more important (and valuable) than "price." If the value is not there, the price is irrelevant. <u>You'd want to find a new accountant immediately</u>. And by the same token, if you ARE experiencing tremendous value (MEANING: you clearly see the benefit of the money you are spending on professional accounting and tax services), then price is also not much of an issue.

You see, we believe our tax business, *by far*, offers MORE VALUE to our clients than the "cost" our services would ever be! And immodestly, we believe we'll do a much better job at ensuring **you receive GREATER VALUE** <u>compared to any other tax professional around</u>!

"Hidden Costs" vs. Price

I've found out the hard way it is a big mistake to try and "blind quote" and give a new client an estimate for work we think we are going to do. Many times once we look at everything, we find out later your tax situation is more involved than anticipated. Since we won't have a good idea of how much tax work will be required until we meet, let's cross that fee bridge when we get there. Again, we are not some ridiculously high-priced tax firm. We are in the middle of the road somewhere when it comes to price, but we're "HIGH" on the Best Accounting & Tax Firm's List when it comes to providing Top Level Peace Of Mind Value for our clients!

<u>Finally, I'd like to make one last comment on this topic of price before we move on</u>. **There are HIDDEN COSTS involved in hiring a cheap and not-so-qualified tax practitioner** to help you deal with the IRS and all of your tax related obligations. These costs are UGLY when they occur, too. BIG Penalties and Cash-Sucking Interest … and, many times, Multiple Years of BACK TAXES you had no idea you owed … plus your time and energy involved in dealing with this kind of IRS crisis – from Day One, until months and years later on when (if) it ends. I've seen this type of business ending catastrophe happen. It is awful.

BOTTOM LINE: It's just not worth it.
You lose your life to this tax burden … a constant distraction,
and in the end (when the IRS agents leave or stop calling and

your cash is wiped out) **Most Businesses Do NOT Recover!**

....

Now can you see how I painted a picture in my sales copy. I'm shaping expectations in the marketing message and "weeding" out the kinds of people that aren't going to use the accounting services anyway.

By writing your sales copy this way, it actually makes your target client feel even more compelled to use you compared to someone else because the copy talks directly to where "he's living!"

Positioning Your Marketing Message

The positioning of your client's mind is where the battle is won or lost. If your client has it in their mind that you only do high-priced tax returns, and they are not looking for high priced tax returns, you're going to have a hard time getting that business.

By the same token, if your client sees you as only a "get your money back fast, assembly line" tax business, and they want somebody that'll spend an hour with them going over some extra tax advice for the coming year, then that client is not going to come in and do business with you.

The positioning in the client's mind is critical -- especially after you have established a reputation about what you do. You may offer a certain kind of service to one group from January to February 15th and then you might start advertising a different way from February 15th all the way to the end of April.

That's how my business was built. We targeted specific groups and advertised to small niches instead of doing mass "image" advertising. Since we targeted "individual" smaller markets, only a selected group of people saw what we do. This way we POSITIONED each group to think about and hopefully respond to the marketing message we put in their heads. (Not some other ad they saw where we are offering totally different benefits to a totally different market!)

I see many tax business owners trying to "be everything to everybody." They will list a variety of tax services all through their ads. The problem is the client doesn't feel like you are talking to him. In his mind, you just "do everything."

If he sees an ad talking about, just "quick tax" services and how fast he can get his money back, AND THAT'S WHAT HE WANTS, he'll feel you are talking directly to him. You have positioned yourself in his mind to be the tax firm that can DO what he's looking to do.

This mistake the tax business owner makes by not positioning himself properly can be traced back to NOT FOCUSING IN ON WHAT HE DOES WELL IN THE FIRST PLACE AND NOT KNOWING WHO HIS TARGET MARKET REALLY IS.

But once this first priority is taken care of, you must start thinking about the **congruency** and **consistency** of your message.

Think about it. If you are "positioning" yourself as a $500/hour tax attorney, you better not have a "cheesy" rug in your lobby. The message is not congruent.

By the same token, your message better be consistent! If in one sales letter you are "pitching" how much time you spend with each individual client and how much more ongoing help you offer year-round, but in another sales letter to the same market you are "pitching" FAST REFUNDS and GET YOUR MONEY BACK QUICK WITH NO FEES PAID UP FRONT!...well.

I hope you can see that there is a consistency problem here.

And, finally, if you want to win the "battle of positioning" in your client's mind, you must keep hammering home YOUR advantage you have over your competition! (USPs!)

If you don't have any good reasons for your target market to choose you compared to your competition, I question whether or not you should be in the tax business altogether!

How To Pick and Use Advertising Media

Real marketing is Market, Message, then Media, in that exact order!

Not ... Media--then figuring out what you want to say (Message) and then figuring out to whom you are going to say it (Market) and then hopefully somebody "bites." That's the exact opposite of what you're supposed to do.

This fatal mistake is made much too often by the regular tax business owners. Why? Well, they just don't know any better. (That's good for you because you've got this book and THEY don't!)

When they choose Media first, it's a recipe for disaster! Their marketing plan's promotional chances for success are fading like a Key West sunset.

You see, if you are following what I'm telling you to do with all of these promotional secrets, and you do them in the PROPER ORDER, the way I tell you to do, your chances for a successful advertising campaign INCREASE considerably!

Don't forget the order of the 3 Ms: MARKET, MESSAGE and MEDIA.

Now let's get into some of the specific secrets to using the different media options that will be available to you.

Does Your Media Actually REACH Your Target Market?

What good is a quality target market for your tax services if you CAN'T reach them?

You could have the "hungriest market" in the United States, but if you can't REACH them with your sales message, you probably need to consider looking for a new target market.

OK, let's say you've found a "hungry market" in your town. It happens to be the city police department and "other community police forces" like them in the surrounding area.

(We have a Member that specializes in this target market and she ends up getting even higher word of mouth referrals than normal tax businesses because cops KNOW EVERYBODY and they talk up her office accordingly!)

The message is:

1. "We specialize in police and other professional service occupations within a 25 mile radius of our office"

2. "My husband is a police officer, I understand the problems people in 'professional occupations' have" (affinity)

3. "20% OFF for new clients in a local professional service occupation, plus LARGE cash rewards for referring their co-workers"

ARE YOU SEEING THE WAY TO GO AFTER A NICHE MARKET HERE?

All right, she's got the first two Ms right (market and message); now what about MEDIA?

She found this group was REACHABLE in a few different ways. (She tried all of them, as you should if you can afford it.)

First, she advertised in the quarterly "professional" journal that hit the streets right before tax season started and right at the end before

April 15th.

Second, she passed out fliers and coupons at the annual Christmas party in December with "early bird" incentives.

And third, she was able to get her hands on a mailing list that she mailed multiple times during tax season.

I don't know her latest numbers, but when she last checked in, this little "niche" market had become extremely profitable for her in just three tax seasons. (In addition, her tax practice receives a higher percentage of word of mouth business within these departments, too.)

She was able to REACH her target market effectively and her numbers speak for themselves!

So how are YOU going to use this simple example to increase your tax business this year? (The formula is easy to follow!)

Strategy #14

Real Media ROI Tips

If you owned a small tax business, located in a small town, and you had $100,000 to spend on advertising, do you think you could get your message seen, read, or heard by your target market?

I'm confident, if you spend six figures advertising your marketing message to a small town, you could definitely reach your target market. However, the problem is you would NEVER make any money!

Number one, the market size wouldn't justify spending that kind of money.

And number two, since you would be wasting 90% of your advertising dollars on prospects NOT interested in your tax services, you wouldn't be able to prepare enough tax returns to offset the expenses.

The bottom line: "You gotta turn a profit if you're gonna stay in business!" (and as an accountant, I'm sure you understand this! ☺)

But the same holds true for your MEDIA selection. It is NOT about "response rates", despite what you may think!

So your sales-to-expense numbers play a very important role in your overall marketing equation. Like Dan Kennedy says, "Your numbers don't lie. If you've got bad numbers, you've got bad numbers."

(Sounds like something Yogi Berra would say, doesn't it?)

Your market and your message may be right, BUT IF YOUR MEDIA IS NOT AFFORDABLE (MEANING IT'S NOT PROFITABLE), EVERYTHING IS STILL WRONG.

Check out this example comparison, using round numbers to show you the role of math in media.

Example:	Val - Pak Coupon vs.	Direct Mail Sales Letter
Reach	10,000 homes	10,000 homes
Cost per	.05	42 postage; .18 printing; piece including misc. = .60 TOTAL
Total exp.	$500	$6,000
Unit sales	10	25
Total Sales	$1,000	$2,500
Gross Profit (@$100 each)	$500	($3,500)

In this particular scenario, I'd choose the Val-Pak coupon over the direct mail sales letter. That doesn't mean I'd always choose an ad in a coupon mailing to a direct mail piece.

What it means is, if I'm checking my numbers properly, I'm going to lean towards trying the media that will make me a net profit on the front end first.

I've kept some media running at a loss, knowing I'll make it up in profit on the back end (i.e. Referrals, "lifetime value" of a client, etc.).

For now, just remember: If the media you choose can't make money or isn't affordable, then look elsewhere for a more cost-effective one.

Media Mindset Keys

Here's the reality: every ad you run will NOT succeed! But that's all right, if you get what I'm about to tell you...

You see, TESTING ads first is one of the most important "secret weapon" strategies a tax business owner can learn. Testing any and all of your marketing plans ahead of time (before you "roll it out" altogether) protects you from making BIG mistakes. Testing also helps you secure the life-blood of your business -- CASH.

Whatever you do, DON'T think that you now are armed with all of this new marketing knowledge, every promotion you try is going to hit a home run!

That's crazy. I have promotions where I get bad results and lose money EVERY tax season! But nine times out of 10 it's with a "test" ad. You see, test ads are just a way to see whether your ad has a chance of working or not.

<u>Note: I use easy to multiply round numbers in my examples to make my points.</u>

I obviously want you to charge MUCH more than $100 for your tax services.

If you spend $100 on a small display ad in the newspaper and you get two clients from the ad (or $200 in revenue) that means your test did 2-to-1. (For every dollar you spent in advertising, you received $2 in sales. That's pretty good.

So now you might try testing a larger ad. This time you place an ad that costs $500 in the same newspaper, running the same day of the week and placed on the page in about the same area as before. The reason for all of this is to keep as many variables the same as possible to get the truest test you can. They are never perfect, but you'll get a good idea.

This time you got ten new clients equaling $1,000 or $500 gross profit, still a 2-to-1 sales to expense ratio. But with the bigger ad, you got eight more clients, plus you made $400 more on the front end. You'll make even more on the back end with more clients now in your database.

Now that you've had two successful tests, you want to run a full page ad. Since the timing is not going to be the same during tax season as the first two successful tests, you're not sure if you should "shell out" the big bucks! (Full page costs $3,500)

This is a good point. Some tax business owners would stay "small" for now and roll out full page ads the following tax season.

But for this example, let's say you go for it. The full page test ad (notice even a full page ad can be a test) runs, and you get 35 new clients. (Break-even @ $100 per client.) Was the test ad successful? In my opinion, it was the most successful ad of the three. Why? Because I got 35 new clients in my database for FREE. (Costs $3,500; Sales $3,500; Net Profit $0; 35 new clients: no cost.)

Now I've got 35 new paying clients, and a high percentage will come back to me year after year and refer a certain number of their friends and co-workers to me as well. I'll make much more profit in the long run with the full page ads running at break-even, than small ads making $500 with a few extra clients.

Don't be afraid to lose some money every now and then when you are testing to find a winner. A "winner" could be an ad in that same newspaper. Let's say you tested the $500 ad and got 30 new clients or $3,000 in sales (6-to-1 sales to ad expense). That's a winner. I'd go full page ASAP (all things considered) and try to get as close to a 6 to 1 ratio again as possible.

As you increase the sizes of your test ads, remember this general rule: The BIGGER the ad, the worse your sales to expense ratio will be. But the good news is, the BIGGER the ad, the better your overall gross profit margins will be.

Every business owner that is a SERIOUS marketer loses money on different types of new promotions they try. Losing money on test ads is part of the marketing process! If you test ten different media with your ad and seven fail, two barely make money, and one is a clear winner, then you hit the jackpot!

Now you take all the money you were going to spend in ten different media ads and put 80% in YOUR HOME RUN and the other 20% split up in a re-test of the two ads that barely made money. (You can tweak 'em and see if they can become more profitable.)

But the moral of this story is, TEST EVERY PLACE YOU THINK MAKES SENSE. Once you track your results and find the money-makers, take the majority of your marketing dollars and invest them in the tests where you received GOOD RESULTS!

This is not rocket science. It is a systematic way for you to eliminate the bad and increase the good in your overall marketing plan!

It may be very surprising to you, but this is how direct-response marketing is really done: it's all a numbers game after a while. And that—my accountant friend—means that YOU are set up for success!

About "Breaking Even" (This Might Shock You)...

If you are trying to increase your tax business, the main thing you should be concerned with in the beginning is market share. You want to get as many people in your tax office as possible as early in the tax season as possible, too.

We've talked about this before. The momentum you build from your client flow is very important. Because we are in "service" business, the more people you have in your business going through your normal "operational funnel," the better. More people refer more new clients. More people means more repeat business the following tax season or throughout the year. The more people in your tax office, the better.

So what do we do to get as many people in our office as possible? Of course we are going to advertise our tax business and promote the 3 Ms like we've already said. The bigger question is, "HOW DO YOU KNOW IF YOUR ADVERTISING IS WORKING?"

That might sound like an easy answer: You know your ad is working when you are making money. True, but let's look closer.

Did you know 80% of the businesses in this country LOSE money when they acquire new clients? How can they stay in business? It's this thing called BACK END sales. (I'll talk about the "back end" until I'm blue in the face, or when everyone in my membership understands and is cultivating it properly in their own tax office -- whichever comes first!)

Back end sales includes everything you sell a client AFTER they use your services the first time. The FIRST sale is always the hardest. After that your marketing to that client gets much easier!

Translate that to the tax preparation industry. We only have ONE sale (for the most part) per year. Can we afford to "lose" money on the front end in order to receive the benefits of the majority of those clients coming back the following year and then multiple years after that, giving us money for ongoing tax services? If you have a big enough bankroll you can.

If you wanted to, you could "BUY" your clients with your advertising. You'd lose money for a couple of years, but build your client base and enjoy the repeat business and ongoing referrals! You would be very profitable in a few years. But here's the way WE did it.

Our goal was to break even on each ad that we'd run. If an ad costs $500, I wanted to bring in five clients to pay for it. The way

I looked at it, I JUST GOT FIVE NEW CLIENTS FOR FREE! "They are in my database and now I'm going to help stimulate the Word-of-Mouth (WOM) Process, and I'm going to send them follow up mailings in the future to make sure they come back, year after year!"

What does the normal tax business owner say after they run an ad that costs $500 and they got only five clients? "I didn't make any money. I'm not running that ad again!"

It's too bad. If more tax business owners understood the VALUE of getting NEW clients in their door at NO ADDITIONAL COST to the owner, there would be much more money in the bank accounts of people in the tax profession in this country.

Now don't get me wrong, I like MAKING MONEY ON THE FRONT END, TOO! If I can get five new clients AND make a few hundred dollars, of course I'd rather go down that road.

The "bigger idea" I want you to understand is, **BREAK-EVEN MEANS FREE CLIENTS!**

How To Multiply Your Media Success

As I mentioned in the previous step, getting more clients into your tax business is simply a numbers game. If you've got a certain headline, advertising pitch, irresistible offer or a combination of them all working in four different kinds of media, you want to do everything in your power to find four MORE media vehicles that make money (and four more, and four more, etc.).

The more tests you run, the more "winners" you find. The more proven ads you can continuously run, THE MORE SALES YOU MAKE, THE MORE YOU INCREASE YOUR OVERALL TAKE-HOME INCOME!

The "catch" for those in the tax-prep-only biz (who don't do year-round write-up work), is that there are only a FEW WINDOWS of opportunity to "make the sale" (or get the client into your office) because, once they commit or file their return, you can't do anything with them for a whole year!

This has its good and bad points. First, the bad: When you test multiple ads this tax season, by the time you get all of your numbers tallied the window of opportunity could be over for that particular target market because they may want to file their taxes at a certain time during the tax season only. This means if you have a big "hit" this year, you'll have to wait until next tax season to go after that same market on a much bigger scale.

Now the good news! Let's say you tested "many fishing lines" this tax season and found out that a majority of them are and should be profitable for the same time next tax season (using the same media and the same or better "pitch" etc.). This is how you grow your tax business fast!

You "parlay" your money on all the test ads that worked last year. Plus, you can roll the dice a little and put some money behind ads that involve the same media, market, message, and timing and roll those out at the same time.

Your goal initially should be to add MARKET SHARE to your client base. Even if your profit margins aren't as high as you'd like, that's OK. The more ads you run, the more times your phone will ring and the more clients will come through your door. You build a MOMENTUM EFFECT that feeds on itself.

People see how much business you are doing, so they want to come find out what all the "fuss" is about. People naturally want to "be a part" of the popular place to go, so you'll get business from people who hadn't even planned on doing business with you; but since you've attracted lines of people, they want to join the group, too.

It's the same idea as when the economy is good, the rich get richer. Well, when business is good, more people are going to want to do business with you instead of the guy down the street by himself hoping to help someone with their taxes. No one is using him, so why would anyone trust that guy?

Since marketing is a numbers game, spend your time each tax season testing more new ads, trying to find more money makers so you can go full throttle the next tax season!

One last thing. What's the number one reason why a tax business owner won't test multiple (maybe ten or fifteen) different ads? The answer is laziness. I know, I've been there.

It's much easier to find three media vehicles that make you money and just stick with those each year. But if you want to double or triple your business FAST, you must find some "other" media to test in and then roll out the winners.

And, if you don't want to do a little extra work this tax season to make NEXT year's promotions that much more profitable, that's your business.

That's what's great about this country. You can choose to grow your own business as quickly or as slowly as you want. What a deal!

The VERY FIRST MEDIA You Should Uses

Without a doubt, the first media to always start with is a sales letter to your own clients. When I do consultations with people, this is the first place I tell them to start.

They want to start out and go after this market and then target that market, and I say, "Wait a minute! You have to tap into the goldmine already right under your nose."

They will say, "Oh, I already send my clients a Christmas card." Or, "Don't worry, they get a postcard from me each year in the first week of January!"

This in my opinion is a terrible waste of existing assets and resources.

Yes, I said ASSETS! Your database IS the top asset in your office. More so than your money in the bank. More so than the computers or your office space.

Let's say you've got 400 clients that came into your office and did business with you last year. Did you know that mailing the right sales letter "reminding" them how great you are and why they came to you last year, updating them on your "story" and what's new for this tax season, AND MOST IMPORTANTLY, giving them some extra incentive to refer others to your tax business, **COULD INCREASE YOUR CLIENT BASE BY AS MUCH AS 10% TO 15% WITH JUST ONE SALES LETTER!**

It's true. And to think you wouldn't take advantage of those 400 potential sales reps already out there in your community just waiting to have an extra few reasons to talk about you to their friends. Don't let that kind of word of mouth business go untapped!

We are in a service business. Service businesses historically "live" off of word of mouth income. Why not "fan the flames" even more and do more than just LIVE? How about increase your income drastically!

I don't know why I have to continue to hammer this point home all the time, but some tax business owners still think the extra expense of a few mailings in January costs too much. It might cost you a few extra dollars in "up-front cash flow" in the early part of tax season, but it is well worth your time, effort, and money, bringing new clients and an increase in your income during the overall tax season!

Most tax business owners still don't "get it" when I say the BACK END part of your tax business is the most profitable! For example, a "dual incentive" Special Refer-A-Friend Plan to increase the "talking up" that goes on between friends, associates, and/or neighbors. That IS part of your back end business.

The front end is obviously getting new clients. (It can get expensive.)

If you're doing a good job in your tax business, you will automatically get referrals. But that's neither the best part nor the most profitable part of your back end. It's the repeat clients that we all get each year. The lifetime VALUE of your clients should be a mandatory study for every tax business owner.

If you went out and measured how much money you actually made from an ad you ran ten years ago, it'd boggle your mind. (That's the REAL back end.)

And if you keep in touch with your clients throughout the offseason in some capacity (a newsletter, regular mailings, occasional gatherings, etc.)…well, that's what will take it up even another notch!

Strategy #18

Your Tax Office Is One Big Sales Media—So Take Advantage Of <u>Every</u> Opportunity!

I want you to mentally "step outside your business" for a minute and take a different kind of look at it with me. I want you to think with me for a second of the "complete business flow" that goes on in your tax office.

> A prospect sees your ad in the yellow pages. (<u>Or the new yellow pages … GOOGLE</u>.) He calls your office and decides to make an appointment. He comes down to your office and is greeted by the receptionist. He waits in the lobby for a few minutes and goes back to meet with a tax preparer. Since he has all his correct tax related information, the preparer decides to finish the return right there as the client watches.
>
> The tax return is complete in less than an hour, and the preparer takes the return to a processor and tells the client it will be about fifteen minutes to review the return, make copies, and have all the paperwork ready for him to sign. The receptionist, processor and tax preparer all thank him for his business as the tax service is completed. The client picks up the return, signs it, and pays for everything. You electronically file it and now your client's "tax obligations" are finished for the year.

That's a pretty standard tax office flow. Your office will be a little different than that, one way or the other, but here's what I want you to notice.

There are SELLING and MARKETING opportunities in every tax office's normal business flow.

The way a receptionist makes eye contact and greets a person when they first walk in makes a difference. What brochures or fliers are available as the client waits? Does the tax preparer make the new client "feel" taken care of? (That is more marketing than you realize.) Does the referral plan get pitched properly either during or once the tax return is completed? How about the processor giving quality assurance the tax return has been double checked for peace of mind? And finally, what back end stimulation procedures are in place to increase referrals? (i.e. Free gifts, a thank you letter, etc.)

Do you see this as ONE BIG SALES PROCESS or "FUNNEL?" You have your tax client in your office and you take the opportunity to "funnel" the client from one place to the next in your office with the whole purpose of increasing your overall back end and long term business.

Now imagine: What if you had an even BIGGER funnel over top of your tax office. And you knew from past experience that for every ten people you added and funneled through your tax office, seven of them would come back the following tax season, and of those seven, four would remain in your client base at least five years. And you also knew that those same initial ten people over a five year period would refer a total of twenty new people to your tax business.

So what's the question you should be asking? ...

"HOW CAN I GET AS MANY PEOPLE AS I CAN IN THAT HUGE FUNNEL ABOVE MY OFFICE AND RUN THEM THROUGH MY "INNER OFFICE" FUNNEL AS EARLY IN THE TAX SEASON AS POSSIBLE?"

This may seem to be an obvious goal, but here's why I am making such a big deal about this: *it's all about radical simplification.*

Look, part of this "49 Lessons" Process is to turn you into a

Marketing Expert, especially relative to other tax business owners. But here's the little secret of top marketers everywhere: they do everything they can to keep things simple! And this is an easy way to conceive of your business…and it affects how you select your media!

So when you advertise and promote your tax business, never forget this "funnel" technique.

If you do, you're just leaving money on the table for some other tax business to have.

Moving From "Internal" (House List) Media To "External" (New Client Acquisition) Media

You've mailed your existing clients multiple sales letters. You have reminded them and re-sold them on the fact that your tax business is their best option AGAIN this tax season.

You even have given them incentives to find you more clients. So you've got the INTERNAL media covered for now. Now let's look at the EXTERNAL.

What is INEXPENSIVE MEDIA? Well, to you, inexpensive may be one price for an ad and to someone else, inexpensive means a totally different figure. Inexpensive is not a relevant term because we all are in different situations and different phases of our growth.

Remember:
I use easy to multiply round numbers in my examples to make my points.
I obviously want you to charge MUCH more than $100 for your tax services.

Another way to look at it is COST vs. SALES. If you ran a new ad and the price was $1,000, but you got nine new clients (or $900 in revenue), the COST of that ad was basically $100 bucks. If every time you run that ad, you lose $100, but you pick up nine new sales, some tax practitioners are going to call that an EXPENSIVE AD while others will say it's inexpensive.

The tax business owner that can lose money every time he runs an ad and is happy to pick up new clients has a good back end system working for him and he knows he'll turn a nice profit down the road. Most tax business owners I talk to don't want to do that. They might not have the money to carry them for a few years, or they just haven't tested out their numbers for what they can count on with regards to their back end sales. That's OK.

So where should we start with in our external advertising? Depending on how much money you have to invest, you should test as many "low priced" media vehicles as you can (that make sense for your target market) and find out which ones break even or make you some money on the front end. I'd also find one or two "more expensive" media which have the potential to attract larger numbers of clients to your office.

Once you've done both the small and the large "tests," track your results, count your money when the dust settles, and plan accordingly for your next wave of ads.

My Favorite "First" Media For a New Office

When we expanded into a new location in a new city, I liked to find out ahead of time what media options were going to be available to me. (Remember: If you can't REACH your target market with your message, what good is it?)

When I speak to tax business owners, one of the most-asked questions is "What are the best ways to advertise a tax business?" Or, "What are the most effective advertisements that get you the most new clients?"

Do you see the problem with their question? They are asking about MEDIA first! They should be asking about that last, with MARKET and MESSAGE ahead. You and I know that, but they don't have this Crash Course at their disposal!

But since I can't tell them ALL of these "49 Lessons" ahead of time and answer their questions properly, I give them somewhat of a correct answer. It goes something like this:

For the purpose of this example, I've done my research, and I know my target market exists in this town, and I think it's a pretty hungry market, but I won't find out for sure until I start my test ads during tax season.

If I'm starting out brand new, going into a city for the first time and opening up a new tax office, I want to know a couple of things about the media.

First, I look for local and national coupon book or magazine direct mail vendors. Historically speaking, they can get me in a group of homes (usually selected by zip codes) for about a dime a piece (or less than six cents if I do volume). You usually have to mail a minimum of 10,000 homes and sometimes more if it's a local vendor, but overall this is extremely inexpensive compared to your potential return on investment.

If the city has two or as many as five or six different coupon vendors competing in that market, that's even better. You get more options for mail dates and different-sized sales pieces for varying messages. Best of all, more competition brings cheaper prices for the consumer -- you and me!

So basically, I'd tell those tax business owners that are asking, use media advertisers like Val-Pak, Money-Mailer, Mail Marketing, Creative Publishers, etc. You'll get more bang for your buck and usually a high number of new clients to boot!

Sometimes when I give this answer, one of them will say, "Oh I've tried that kind of advertising before. It never worked for me." To that guy I say, maybe the problem is NOT with the media. Maybe it has to do with your market or message.

He'll say, "What do you mean by that?"

And I say, "You'll have to join our membership group."
(I can't give out free advice forever. ☺)

Then another tax business owner will chime in saying, "Well, I target high-end taxpayers, and they never use those cheap coupon mailers!" To him I say, "You do what you want. I can only talk from experience with my own tax business and helping other tax business owners in my membership group. I've used this form of media to land high-end clients for our Executive Tax Service business, and I've helped others do the same, so I can more than likely do it for you."

(Some become members and some don't. It's a free country.)

A Media "Check-List"...

When I sit down to plan my marketing strategy for the coming year, these are the media options I look at first to see what's available for each individual market where our tax offices are located.

In order of priority, the media vehicles are:

- ☐ existing client sales letter (w/ referral slips)
- ☐ existing client follow up sales letter (w/ more referral slips)
- ☐ existing client reminder post card
- ☐ thank you note and cash reward letter
- ☐ yellow page ad (updated) ... and of course new GOOGLE ads
- ☐ direct-response (not "brand-building" or brochure style) website
  - Search Engine Optimization (SEO)
  - Pay Per Click (PPC)
  - Banner Ads
  - Internet Endorsement
  - Email Marketing
- ☐ banner, your business' sign (other "attention getting drive by" ideas)
- ☐ national coupon book (or magazine) vendors
- ☐ local coupon book (or magazine) vendors
- ☐ W-2 coupon inserts into company envelopes
- ☐ newspaper inserts (daily paper)
- ☐ news "rag" paper insert (weekly paper)

- ☐ register tape coupons (grocery stores near our location)
- ☐ new homeowner sales letter
- ☐ new business owner sales letter
- ☐ coupon fliers (target niches)
- ☐ posters & flier coupons (high traffic locations)
- ☐ newspaper classified ads
- ☐ newspaper display ads (advertorial only)
- ☐ press releases (newspaper, TV, radio)
- ☐ TV ads
- ☐ radio ads
- ☐ bus ads
- ☐ billboard ads

This list gets me started. Different towns will have different kinds of vendors with different opportunities to use some, part, or none of these media options listed. In some markets I know certain media will work better than others because I've been testing for years. You'll learn the same about what media are more effective in your neck of the woods in due time.

This list will help check to make sure you are not MISSING anything major!

Insider Tricks In Specific Media
(Part 1)

The First Thing You Should Know About Different Media Types…

Once you've got a good handle on your market and your message, you're going to want to find as many media vehicles as possible and see if you can make them work. (That's determined by whatever sales-to-expense ratio you're willing to live with and feel you can be profitable with over the long haul.)

Let's say you have seven different ads running in seven different media outlets. In this example, the most profitable dollars and overall the most new clients are coming from two main sources. One is a local coupon magazine media and the other is a national coupon card deck.

Since you are hitting "home runs" with these two ads in these two media, try taking the same message and layout of these coupons and making them into "flier inserts" to test in other media vehicles.

The first place I'd start would be in an inexpensive place like a weekly "rag" magazine or newspaper. They have low circulation and in some cases you can really hit certain target markets at a very cheap overall rate.

Why try inserts when you could place the same message and layout in a display ad?

Well, you can! But, from my experience, "bright colored, odd shaped" fliers get more attention (and correspondingly get read more), which in the long run brings more sales. The display ads will work, especially if you are using "advertorial" techniques. I'm just saying try the inserts first.

"RECYCLING" your marketing will help see if your headlines will "pull" in other areas. Sometimes after I have tested the same ad with two different headlines and I didn't get any change in response, I'll recycle those same headlines and run them in other media to see if it makes a difference.

You'll find out your "hot headlines" better this way. I've even recycled my hottest headlines and added them to my yellow page ad. (You don't want to put unproven headlines or ad copy in your yellow page ad. A year is a long time to wait when it's not "pulling!")

Yellow Pages Ads

<u>NOTE:</u> *Since Google is the new yellow pages,* some tax pros stopped using yellow page advertising. My answer to the question of whether to continue investing in yellow page advertising is simple. They are really cheap now. So if you have an opportunity, test it in your area with a special phone number that forwards to your main tax office. <u>Find out for sure how many leads are actually calling your tax business twelve months of the year. Then make a decision based on facts and revenue generated from these yellow page inquiries.</u>

Many tax business owners tell me the yellow pages are too expensive for what you get these days. Or they tell me they don't want to pay an advertising expense year-round for just a seasonal business. Well, let me tell you right up front how DUMB that really is!

Look, if you think this way, too, listen up. First of all, as we have discussed before, "expense" is relative. You take the price of a yellow page ad and compare that to your sales that came directly from that same ad, and what do you have?

If you have a good ad, you AT LEAST break even. So again I say,

"That ad WASN'T expensive! It DIDN'T COST YOU a dime!"

Now take your total annual yellow page price (x) and then take your total seasonal sales from the ad (y), put them together. Once you compare annual versus seasonal, you can make a real educated decision.

OK, now that you are on the right track, look at your local yellow page book. Go ahead and take it out now, I'll wait. (Ready?)

All right, what are all the other tax business owners doing in there? How do they compare to you and your ad? Are you "in column" or running a display ad? How many display ads are listed? Who are they targeting? Are they going after the same target market you are? Are any of their locations close to yours?

These are just some of the questions you should be asking as you decide how large you should make your new yellow page ad before the coming tax season. You should eventually look to be THE dominant ad in the yellow pages under your heading. (i.e. Tax preparation, accountants, CPAs, bookkeeping, etc.)

Why? Yellow page advertising for people in the tax industry is almost as important as yellow page advertising is for plumbers and people in other service industries. With the most dominant ad with the right message, targeting the right market; a new tax business can grow extremely fast within two or three tax seasons, from that one yellow page ad alone.

Eighty-eight percent of the people looking under a "tax heading" will notice or look at (and hopefully read, if your ad's good) the most dominant ad on the page. Now THAT is a lot of possible prospects calling your tax office to inquire about your tax services. (If you or your staff can't answer the phone properly and sell "getting an appointment," your yellow page advertising dollars will be wasted! Don't make that mistake.)

Yellow page advertising is like every other form of advertising. The main draw back with the yellow pages (for tax prep businesses) is you get ONE shot! If your ad stinks, you've got to wait a whole year to change it. So how do you protect yourself from running a lousy ad? Use proven ads that have already tested out well for you and get you a high response rate.

How much should you increase your ad presence in the yellow page book? It depends on how much of a risk taker you are.

Either way though, over time have the goal of increasing your ad size and testing the response during each tax season. Eventually, you'll be THE (or one of the) dominant ads!

Your Office Location (That's a "Media" Too)

Every tax business has some kind of "location" (even if it's home and you're working out of your garage.) And every location has some kind of sign saying, "XYZ Tax Service."

The secret to helping your location bring in more new clients is to, whatever you do, MAKE SURE IF SOMEONE COMES BY IT, THEY WILL AT LEAST NOTICE IT!

You could have an excellent location or a not so good location. Either way make sure whoever goes by sees you ARE a tax service business and you can offer them (blank). It should be one of your short USPs.

You see, not only do you want to get noticed, but you also want to be constantly SELLING or marketing yourself. A large banner with something like "Worry-Free Service" hanging below your company sign, keeps that marketing message out in front of any "passers by" 24 hours a day, 7 days a week.

I have a client that keeps her Christmas lights up all the way through April 15th. She says people driving by her office notice her better. She even has special lights on her banner to make it stand out even more! How does she know the lights work?

Easy -- she asks new clients how they heard of her. One third of them say, "Well, I saw your lights and decided to come give you a try." (I'd say that the lights and the lit banner do a pretty good job!)

If you feel your location just isn't right and it may be time to make a change, here's a few things to remember...

1. **Anytime you change locations, you will lose a few clients** because they will not be smart enough to find you -- I don't care how many letters you send them. (One year we moved one of our locations next door fifty feet away from our previous location, and we got more phone calls than I thought from clients asking where we moved.)

    We sent them letters, and a big fat poster was on the door of our old location pointing right to our new office, and people STILL got confused.

2. **Go where your target market is.** Get office space near where they live or work or around the high traffic areas where they shop. Don't try and promote your tax services to a blue collar market from a high rise location on the twelfth floor. (You'll be fighting an uphill battle in all your ads!)

    For that market, I'd go find a little strip mall near where they live with a high traffic flow visible to your office. If you can afford it, set up next to a Wal-Mart or big high volume "discount" grocery store.

    But most of all, targeting lower income markets, go get as close to H & R Block's office as you can.

    Yes, believe it or not—that's a SMART strategy! Why not scoop up all the folks that are frustrated by a long wait or poor service? It's also a great shortcut to figure out office location.

Endorsed Mailings

Everybody knows somebody! And I know without asking you, you've got contacts with someone who can endorse you.

You've got people you know in your church. You've got people at your kids' school, like the principal. You know someone with some influence who works in a large office complex. (And these people may not even be your clients. They just may be personal friends who have a little influence in their area they live or work in.)

Once you've written down everyone you can think of on that list, sit back with a cup of coffee and go through your existing client files. All you will have to do is look at the 1040 or the notes in the file and you'll remember who this person was. Some of them (you'll remember) were very appreciative of your services. A few even sent you a thank you note and an unsolicited letter saying how much they thought of you and the service you gave them.

Now take your best five or ten, call them and say you'd like to do a mailing to a group of people they know (with whom they have some "sphere" of influence) and have them ENDORSE you and your tax business. Most people would be flattered you asked them. (You are putting them up on a "pedestal" and pumping up their pride a little just by bringing up the subject.)

If you want, you can even offer them a 10% to 20% cut off of whatever sales come from their specific mailing. (If they are your friend, don't worry about offering it. If it's someone you don't know that well, go ahead and offer it up front.)

You will pay for the all the printing, the postage and the labor involved in putting it all together. You can even write the letter for the "endorser" to sign so they don't have to do ANY work. They'll read it, of course and make any changes necessary, but this way the person you pick gets a "no brainer" deal. You pay for everything. You do all the work. They get a "piece of the action" just for saying you're a great guy!

The mailing that will go out will be your basic sales letter changed a little to target whatever group it's going to. The cover letter will be on your endorser's stationary, using their envelope with their "recognizable" name on it. (And that's the key secret.)

The direct mail letter gets opened. Their friend or fellow co-worker is telling them about a great tax professional he knows. The timing hits right when everyone's getting their W-2s and BAM! Don't be shocked if you get double digit response rates. It happens more with "endorsed mailings" than most any other direct mail piece.

Strategy #21

Insider Tricks In Specific Media
(Part 2)

Local Community Publications

These are growing in number all over the country. The big newspapers are failing, but often these little "free" guys are doing very well.

So you can FIND and REACH a lot of small niche markets by promoting your tax business in any of the little local publications that are in and around most medium sized cities. I've advertised in publications that served towns as small as 10,000. So I know you can find some in most areas.

The trick is to test and find out which ones are RESPONSIVE and which ones are not.

If you are a pet lover, you probably have some kind of "pet monthly" publication around your area being distributed to all the other pet lovers. You talk empathetically to them about pets in your ad's sales copy. Then make an offer of something like "20% off tax preparation fees," but the "catch" is a picture of your pet on your coupon. Then you have your "pet wall of fame" in your office and you'll attract even more people from this "pet lovers" niche.

By the way, do you think having a picture of your client's pet hanging in your office is going to help with client retention? You bet! (Tell 'em to bring you an updated picture each year!)

There are other niche groups in your city you can target using these local publications. Health journals, sports papers, beauty mags, business journals, hobbyist publications, etc. -- you name it, you might find it in your area.

Business journals are good publications to try your test ads. You're targeting the business community or the "white collar" professional crowd and you can usually find a "hungry group" in there somewhere.

For this particular monthly journal, let's say they don't take advertising inserts. You say, "That's fine," but here are some quick tips to increase your chances for success:

Good placement is EVERYTHING when you advertise in these kinds of media. If you get stuck on a bottom page, left hand side towards the back, your response is definitely going to go down.

Where is the best placement?

Get as close to the front as you can. Get on a right-hand page if you can. And if at all possible, make it UPPER RIGHT HAND PAGE. The sales rep will give you the same ol' line, "I can't guarantee placement." That's fine.

Start with bringing the layout crew coffee and donuts a couple of mornings a week and see what happens to your placement compared to the other advertisers (who don't bring the goodies).

Hey, a friendly cup of coffee and a donut never hurt anybody. It's amazing how a friendly gesture that costs a couple of bucks will increase your sales numbers so well.

You think this is a small point. I've had placement affect an ad from one week to the next by over $1,500. (That's nothing to sneeze at.)

Co-Op Mailings

I'll tell you right up front, this one will take a little extra work on your part. However, it is an extremely effective way for you to mail out 30,000 to 35,000 pieces of mail in early January with your message on it. Another batch of the same amount with a different message targeting a different group in the middle of February and then finally the same at the end of March promoting to the procrastinators.

That's 100,000 pieces of mail selling to three different target groups, all for FREE!

OK, here's how you do it.

The work you'll be doing is the legwork for setting up a "co-op" mailing. You'll get a couple of restaurants, a couple of pizza places, a carpet cleaner, a pest control business, a car wash business, a dentist, a lawyer, and whoever else you can think of. (I would recommend going to people or business contacts you already know or have some "relationship" with.)

Just go in and tell them you're putting together a mailing with fifteen to twenty other businesses and everyone will have an opportunity to throw a half-page flier into an envelope. Work out the correct "weight and mailing" requirements with your local mailing house. Find out how many half-page ads can fit into a certain sized envelope at a certain weight and then see what his costs would be to set it up and put it together for you.

You can be responsible for getting everyone's ad laid out at a printer's office, too. Just use the same one that will be doing all the printing for you. Then get a total for all their charges and add it to the mailing house expense.

Once you know your total costs, divide it by nineteen businesses and charge them accordingly. You did all the work, so the 20th business is YOURS and you get in the mailing for FREE!

QUICK TIP: Once you make all the contacts (and close all the sales you need) get a high school student or maybe a friend of the family or your "older" kids to do most of the grunt work. You will need to be spending your time running your regular business.

By the way, the best time to get other businesses lined up for this is in October and November. As soon as you get close to the holidays and Christmas, people get too busy or they get too side tracked to be thinking "clearly" about next year's promotions.

Oh, and the best part?

Once you do it the first year, the next few years will be a snap!

How To Find That Elusive "Starving Crowd"

And Tips on "New Homeowner" Letters...

I want to stop to remind you that the BEST kind of media will directly reach the "starving crowd" for your services. This is one of the late, great Gary Halbert's key principles: "I'll forsake EVERY other marketing advantage, but give me a starving crowd for my product, and I'll kick your tail from here to Hoboken!"

So here are some **practical ways to find out which "niche groups" in your area are STARVING for certain types of tax services.**

First of all, if you've been living in your town for any length of time, you kind of have a "feel" for population statistics in your area. You should know about what percentage of people are in lower, middle, and higher income brackets, about where they live in and around the city and other general information.

You should also have a decent idea of who your competition is and what kind of clientele they mostly service. Do they just handle mostly high-end customers? Or do they electronically file a ton of low income returns? And if you have many competitors offering what seems like a full range of tax services, look and see WHERE their offices are located and what sections of the city and surrounding county would be convenient for the different target market groups to use their offices.

Once you've done your homework (if you are not familiar with the town you're in, it will take you a little longer) you might already "see" a few possibilities for some "starving crowd" groups NOT having certain tax services easily available to them because of location or because very few tax business owners are actually offering a particular tax service.

But let's say you are still not sure what "starving" markets might be available to promote different tax services to (you actually never TRULY know until you test anyway), so you want to choose a few media vehicles that you feel will be reachable and affordable for your "hunches."

The media you choose should normally have a way to try and capture taxpayers who may be in TRANSITION. People who have major (or even minor) changes in their tax situation tend to become VERY EAGER to get it straight before the IRS deadline. So what media examples are the best?

Personally, I like to use media that are inexpensive per potential lead. The kind like the coupon decks that will hit a whole section of one side of the city. If I know that side is where most of the lower income folks live, and I'm thinking this is a target market that is not getting serviced properly in this town by H & R Block or other tax businesses targeting the refund loan bank product market, then I'll run some test ads.

The headlines and subheads will be the same proven ones we've been using, but the actual sales copy might talk more about problems they may be having with other tax firms, along with "Here's a deal, come try us this tax season." If it is a hungry market, the phones will ring in our office. (Whenever you find a really hungry market, you'll know it. How? Because your phone calls and normal response rates will go through the roof, and you'll see a pattern of the same calls and new customers coming from the same place.)

The more small, inexpensive tests you do during tax season, the more potential "starving crowds" you may be able to find. The more you find this year, the more money you can invest into reaching them NEXT tax season.

And if you know what groups are in a "feeding frenzy" for what kinds of tax services BEFORE tax season starts next year, you will have a huge competitive advantage over everyone else in your area!

Here's One Starving Crowd...

I know many tax business owners in this country buy and use mailing lists targeted towards new homeowners and new business owners. There are even mailing list firms that do nothing but target other businesses (like us in the tax industry) and try and sell us as many names as we can use. (So there must be a lot of accountants and tax professionals using these lists.)

So what's the main pitch most tax professional use? "Congratulations on your new home purchase. Just welcoming you to town. Here's a coupon for a free consultation." Blah, blah, blah.

Do you think they got a dozen other letters from other service professionals saying about the same thing? You bet they did. (And probably some of them came from the same mailing list firm you got your names from.) **So what can you do that's different?**

First of all, unless you can offer them some kind of tax services on the "off season," DON'T send anybody on your mailing list anything until the first of the year. If you send them a newsletter or a magnet with your name on it, for the most part you are wasting your money.

(Some people will disagree with me on this. That's fine. I'll mail my sales letters during tax season to that same group of new homeowners you've been mailing throughout the summer and fall. At the end of tax season, I'll bet you a steak dinner that my overall mail campaign "hitting during the buying season" NETS more profit than yours, hands down.)

And if you are going to take the time to buy this targeted mailing list (of usually "hungry" taxpayers looking for a new tax professional to help them), then don't just send them one sales letter and that's it! Test as many as three mailings during the tax season: One in the first week of January, One in the middle of February, And the last in the fourth week of March.

What would I say in my sales letter that would be different from what most other tax practitioners would say? Easy. I would and STILL almost always use FEAR selling! (Hey, we've got a built in "scare factor" called the IRS. Why not use it to our full advantage?)

My headlines are going to start off by saying, **"WARNING: New Homeowners!! Uncle Sam is targeting people like you for IRS audits this year!"** Or if a person just started a new business, "WARNING: New business owners must learn the three things that 'red flag' the IRS and guarantee you an audit of your personal and business finances!

Believe me. Using this technique will far outsell saying, "Congratulations on your new home, etc."

Big Mistakes and Success Essentials for Broadcast Media (Radio/TV)

Many tax professionals ask me about radio advertising and whether I think it is effective. My answer is yes, radio ads can be effective, but like anything else you have to test it. So the next logical question comes up, "How do you track radio ads?"

When you do try radio ads, they are hard to track, so one of your goals for the ad needs to be making an offer that's trackable! Number one, if they are a new customer, you are already going to be asking how they heard about you. Hopefully, if the reason is that they heard your ad on the radio, they will tell you.

Secondly, to help the process become easier to track (and actually make a more effective ad) you **make a special offer for radio listeners only.** If they come down to your tax office and say they heard the ad on the radio, you'll give them $27 off tax preparation fees. <u>If you don't find some way to tell whether the radio advertising dollars are working for you, you may be wasting a lot of money.</u>

Our tax business didn't do a whole lot of radio ads. (I guess I'm more of a pure direct-response marketer, so I like to use direct mail media more often than anything else.)

We probably should have spent more time advertising on the radio. Once we determined what to do, we made money every time we tried it in most markets. There was a time in the early '90s when I lost money in almost every case because I was learning by "trial and error." (My loss is, again, now your gain.)

The main thing I learned about radio ads was to pick a certain target audience and a certain time frame and with whatever budget of money you have try to "blow 'em out of the water" all at the same time! Let me explain…

We'll target the RAL market. We'll pick a radio station that hits this market the best in and around your tax office. The window of time is the last ten days of January and the first five days of February. On this station, targeting this market during THE peak of the RAL business, we will run about six or eight radio ads per day for two weeks straight! (On 1/31, 2/1 & 2/2 we'll run ten to twelve ads to completely saturate this market.)

Obviously, the message is built around "Quick Refunds" and getting your money back fast, but the "special radio offer" has a deadline of February 10th only (to help increase the urgency).

So when we use radio, it is in a "quick hit" style, completely saturating the market with specific offers and deadlines and then getting out fast. (Automobile dealerships do a good job of this in their end-of-the-month advertising blitz. That's how I got the idea for our tax business and it works! Remember what I said about taking successful ideas from other industries and testing them in the tax industry.)

Another good time to test a radio advertising blitz is the first two weeks in April! (Yes, go after the those procrastinators!) Advertise on rock stations with male audiences 25 to 45 years old. Many "regular workers" and on the road "sales professionals" are the ones that wait until the last minute.

Run a ton of ads between April 1st and April 14th and blitz the procrastinator market with a special deal, saying, "We've never done this before, we want to see how many of you are really out there, we can't do this crazy promotion forever, Uncle Sam wouldn't let you wait much longer either, etc."

(It's actually kind of fun to see if you can stir up the feeding frenzy even more and really get a lot of people calling and coming down to your office.)

Applying these principles to TV...

When you're using the TV as an advertising medium, you want to test and track the response of your dollars spent here, too. (It's a lot like radio advertising, but with pictures. ☺)

We'll blitz a TV ad at different times of the tax season with different messages in different markets. Again, I am not a huge fan of TV advertising (like radio ads) because you can't track your results as well as "pure" direct response.

Many times TV ads help the other advertising you happen to be running during tax season because of the "combination effect." People won't tell you that they necessarily saw your ad on the TV, but that may have helped them come in after they saw your Val-Pak ad, too! (The combination of your advertising and its effect on your overall response rates is nearly impossible to track. Just count this EXTRA "combination effect" as just gravy if it happens.)

And don't believe the sales rep's line when he says, "You need to get your name out there." You are NOT in business to "get your name out" anywhere! You are in business to make a profit, and you do that by making more DIRECT sales, not by increasing your TV image advertising budget!

You don't have enough money to do image ads. Let Coke, McDonald's or Nike waste their money. Now go back to thinking about ways you can measure the TV spots you spend advertising dollars on using direct response.

I "borrowed" an idea from the hotel industry and used it to make some money in the tax business. (Always keep your eyes and ears open for direct-response ideas you get from other industries' ads! I "snag" ideas from other types of businesses all the time.)

Have you ever seen the Motel 6 TV Commercial where they make it look like they are cutting your TV screen up so you can use a coupon for their hotel? The visual effect of tearing off a coupon from your TV screen is attention getting and it helps make their offer more clear and measurable.

So I did the same type of thing with a local TV station and one of our tax offices. (The special effects weren't as good, but it didn't matter as much.) The target clients got the idea and came into our tax office saying they saw the TV ad and to please give them their $22 discount.

Hey, that sure helped us measure the response better. We might have gotten more clients from the TV ads, but the ones that said they saw it (received the discount) paid for the cost of running those spots by six-and-a-half-to-one. That's $6.50 of gross sales to every $1 spent on the TV ad.

Strategy #24

"Congruence" and Reinforcement

Here's a real simple step that many tax pros MISS:

Use "inner office" brochures and fliers to REINFORCE your external marketing!

Many of our members do a good job getting new clients in the door, but then once the client is THERE, they don't do anything to reinforce the sales message that GOT them there. You want to advertise WITHIN your office...not just outside of it.

A few things you must remember about advertising IN your office.

One, if your clients are ALREADY in your office, your message doesn't need to be (and shouldn't be) the same as the external message you're currently promoting.

Your internal marketing should REINFORCE the same external message but in a different way.

Let's say you have a banner outside your building that reads, "1 Day Tax Preparation Service -- GUARANTEED" (see flier for details).

Why would you do that? Basically, because you can't and shouldn't put your "whole" marketing message up on a 4 x 8 banner. You should make your best marketing USP point clear and simple and then leave rest up to "selling" as you answer their questions or hand them the flier or brochure.

The same holds true in direct mail pieces. Sometimes economics doesn't let you tell your "whole selling story" because you only have a few inches on a Money Mailer coupon, or less space than a four page sales letter.

Saying in your ad or sales letter, "See guarantee flier for details," helps you use more emotional selling phrases the keep your reader in the copy, and then they can logically back up their emotions by reading the details or asking your employees questions.

Your flier might say, "Our guarantee applies to 95% of our clients' tax returns. If you are one of the 5%, then we will tell you upfront that you wouldn't be eligible for our one-day tax service."

That's simple, but you don't want to say all of that in the beginning of your ad. You'd lose sales! That's why you have inner office brochures. Not to sell them again -- they are already there -- but to remind your clients of all the benefits of using you as a tax service and even to "cover yourself" if you have clients complaining about particular features of your services or guarantees.

Strategy #25

Direct Mail "Mini-Series"
(Part 1)

Building a "House List"

Whenever you do a direct mail piece, **the quality of your mailing list makes a huge difference.** An average written sales letter with an average offer mailed to a "HIGH RESPONSIVE" LIST will always out-pull the best written sales letter and the most incredible offer that is mailed to a poor, unresponsive mailing list.

With that in mind, we need to make sure we get our hands on and mail A LOT to "highly responsive lists" of prospects! And what's the best strategy to do this? How about make your own list!?!

You know better than any "mailing house" what your target market wants, where they live, and what their normal patterns are. So it only makes sense you could come up with "something" this target audience wants so they would be willing to give you their name and address in exchange for that thing, right?

Well, I just told you how to make your own RESPONSIVE mailing list. You do it through "lead generation" advertising.

Here's how it works. You run an ad offering a "widget" (something you put together that your target audience would want). It could be a free report, an audio or video tape or whatever you like. You could run a classified ad saying:

WARNING: Before you file your taxes this year, read this Free

Report! "STOP FLUSHING YOUR CASH DOWN THE "IRS" TOILET: 9 Ways To Stop Overpaying Uncle Sam, With No Fear Of An IRS Audit!" Call 1 (800) STOP TAX or write Box 000 Taxville, 12345.

Only qualified prospects are going to take the time to call and get their hands on your free report. Now you've got their name and address, so mailing this group of prospects and pitching them on using your tax services has a much higher chance of being successful!

Wouldn't you want to continue to mail sales material pitching your tax service to a list of these kinds of prospects rather than to a "cold" list that you bought from some mailing house? (I thought so.)

And by the way, if you go through the trouble of getting a few selected taxpayers' names and addresses, don't give up on them early. Just because they didn't respond to your first sales piece doesn't mean they aren't going to respond later.

Test multiple mailings over a period of time. This person IS interested in possibly using your tax services. But the timing might not have been right.

And don't give up on "old" leads. (Periodically you can go back and do a special mailing just to those who responded to your free report over a year ago, but haven't used your tax services yet.)

You will be surprised how many "old" and maybe forgotten leads you can resurrect.

How To Build That List – Easier Than You May Think

Important "money-making" marketing opportunities are wasted every day in your business if you don't have a "name capture" system in place when your phone rings (especially during tax season).

Think about how many people (non clients) call your tax office in a given year "inquiring" about the different tax services you offer. What if you could CAPTURE most (if not all) of the names of those inquirers? What if the normal procedure for answering the phone in your office was that after you answered their question you said, "Would you be interested in a Free Report on this subject?" (Or a free audio CD that explains the topic in more detail.)

Then you could say, "We even include free discount coupons for our services and other related tax services in the packet of info you receive."

Then assume the sale by asking, "And how did you spell your first name?" Then go ahead and take all of their information and get them on your mailing list. You could capture hundreds and even thousands of names over the course of one year's time. You can split test offers and see what kind of person is more responsive to different kinds of offers.

You can even advertise other widgets to this ongoing database, too. Do the same kind of lead generation advertising as we talked about before and offer a free video tape targeting a low end market. They may not want to read a 25-page report, but they would want to watch a thirty minute video on how they can get their refund money back faster!

This way you are constantly trying to break down your database into little "niche" markets, each desiring different kinds of tax services from you. You are doing the same thing with your external advertising, but the difference is this "name captured" list is going to be more responsive than a COLD market that has not called your tax offices before and has NOT asked to receive information from you.

I just want you to see how this DOES make a difference. Dan Kennedy says: "A business without a mailing list isn't a business." Simple and very true.

What are you doing with your business' mailing list?

Strategy #26

Direct Mail "Mini-Series" (Part 2)

This is "Lead Generation" At Its Best

Lead generation marketing can be costly in the beginning, but well worth the expense in the end! When you use lead generation marketing techniques, you are taking your prospect through a "multiple hoop" process. Having a two-three- or more-step marketing strategy, will cost more than a regular "one-step" ad where the prospect calls your office for an appointment.

So, why go the more expensive route?

Well, to properly answer the question, you have to put "expensive" in perspective. (As long as the net profit at the end is high enough, it shouldn't matter necessarily how much the up front or ongoing costs are. Unless, of course, you have a cash flow issue to deal with.)

Once you understand that cost is relative, then to address your question, QUALITY clients is the answer to why you should do multi-step lead generation advertising.

Think about it. You have a prospect that reads your ad, calls your number, and asks for a free report and then responds to whatever your offer is at the end. Since this process takes ten days or so before they call back or come into your office, don't you think that prospect has more "invested" in you and feels more "tied" to your tax business ALREADY than from just seeing an ad and responding the same day.

You want to have as many people as possible in your database that "worked" a little to get there. They are more committed to you and your tax services, and they will refer others much more easily and more quickly when you make them jump through these qualifying steps.

Now you might think $500 bucks is not worth the extra time and "hassle" of managing and following up with an ongoing database. Well, you'd be wrong.

First, that's just one ad. You would be testing many, many during a typical year, especially during tax season. A few hundred dollars multiplied by many ads ADDS UP!

Secondly, and more importantly, you are getting BETTER customers! (In this example you've actually added twice as many clients than one-step advertising, and they are quality!)

Another reason you can "attract" more potential prospects is that it's always easier to get someone to take your "widget" for free, instead of them calling you up to set an appointment to have their taxes prepared. You cut down on the uncomfortable and uneasy sense the client has, feeling like he's going to be sold when he calls your office.

Direct Mail "Mini-Series" (Part 3)

Getting Direct Mail Opened

We all will try different promotions for different target markets offering different messages. In many of these situations we will have to use an envelope to "deliver" the sales message. However, **your sales message is irrelevant if your prospect never opens your letter and looks inside your envelope!** Your envelope is the key to unlocking the sales message for your potential client.

There are two main "camps," or schools of thought, on what's the best way to get your envelope opened so your sales letter has a chance of getting read.

The first one is called "the sneak up approach" or the ol' "A pile vs. B pile" technique.

Basically, the theory is most people open their mail about the same way. When they get the day's mail, they divide it into two piles. Personal mail, bills, subscriptions to their favorite magazines, etc. are placed in the "A" pile, and "unsolicited" letters, catalogs and miscellaneous "junk mail are placed in the "B" pile. (Many times the "B" pile falls straight into the circular file. Go to a post office sometime and watch the people separate their mail over the trash can if you don't believe me.)

One other thing to notice about people dividing up their "A pile and B pile" mail is how the postage is paid. Is the letter stamped or is it bulk rate? Is it first class, third class or, worse, a "to current resident, geographic area bulk rate" metered mail? First class stamps tend to make it over to the "A" pile more often than these other means.

So if your "numbers" and the economics of your promotion allow you to do so, TEST using the sneak up approach when promoting to anyone NOT already your customer. By this I mean use a plain white envelope and HAND ADDRESS the lead's name and address information in addition to your return address. The upper left-hand corner should be your address only. (Do not use your name or company name.) Add FIRST CLASS POSTAGE STAMPS on the envelope and let the postal carriers do their thing.

Taking these steps will get you in the prospect's "A pile." That means your letter WILL get opened and that IS the whole purpose of your envelope (to get your prospect to at least look at the sales letter).

Going back to those postal carriers for a second. Do you think they deliver every piece of mail you send out every day? Whether they deliver it or your letter gets lost or whatever, and depending on who you talk to, a certain percentage of everything in your mail DOESN'T reach the intended recipient. If you are talking second or third class or even bulk rate mailings, now we are really talking large chunks of mail NOT getting delivered!

Why? Some people might say laziness. Other folks might say incompetence. It doesn't matter the reason, if even some of your first class mail DOESN'T get delivered properly, you need to consider your overall mailing options. (Cost of first class mail vs. bulk rate mail)

If you say you can't afford first class postage, then you are probably asking how do you use bulk mailing rates and be effective?

That's the WRONG question to ask! If you think first class postage is too expensive, look at the alternative. How about up to 30% or 40% of your mailing NOT reaching your prospects? Or how about half those people throwing your sales letter away before ever opening it because they saw a bulk rate stamp?

This can get ridiculous! Only a third of your intended prospects opened your envelope. No wonder your response is so low. You think your mailing is getting 100% delivered and 100% opened. (Please don't be naive.)

You talk about expensive. With these kinds of percentages YOU CANNOT AFFORD NOT TO USE FIRST CLASS MAIL! Bulk rate postage is much more expensive if you compare it to response rates of using first class postage.

I've said this before to other tax practitioners, and one in particular came back at me saying, "Well, I've tested both and first class postage lost money just like the bulk rate meter I tried."

I said to him, "Sounds like either a message problem or a market problem to me." You see, if you have a lousy mailing list or a sales message that stinks, then first class postage isn't going to make a hill of beans difference anyway! An old mentor of mine always use to say, "You can't multiply zeros."

Now let's talk about the other "school of thought." Many marketers are solidly on the other side of the camp saying you have to use excellent selling "teaser copy" on the outside of your envelope to help it get opened.

There is some truth to this style or marketing strategy, too. (Heck, just look at the majority of the sales letters that get mailed today -- 95% of them has some kind of "teaser strategy" on the outside of the envelope to help them get opened.)

Personally, I use both strategies. Here's my advice if you want to go this route.

If you are going to "reveal" up front that "this is a sales letter," then by all means, go all out! I mean blanket the whole envelope front and back with multiple bullet points, headlines, subheads, etc. Use some of your best USPs that are in your sales letter on the outside as the teaser copy.

Look, don't hold back! If you are going to "cross the line" in the beginning, then you've GOT to sell them on opening this envelope and that doing so is the best thing since "sliced bread!"

Cover the front. Cover the back completely, too. Maybe even add something on the inside of the envelope to make it look and feel "bulky" so you will pique their curiosity.

Hey, the sky's the limit. Be as creative as possible when you are NOT going to do the plain Jane "sneak up approach."

Both will work. You decide what works best for your situation.

Final Words on Media:
Negotiation and Accountability

Look folks, everything is negotiable. And I mean everything! If some ad salesman tells you this is the best deal you can get, I'd say, "Here's what I'm offering," and negotiate some more.

It is really important to BUY your advertising media at the best price possible. The better deal you get, the more pressure you take off your marketing, and the higher the chances are for success. Just look at it this way. The better the deal you get now, the less sales you have to make for break-even! (Or for a certain profit level, depending on your marketing goal.)

If the price of a newspaper display ad is $750, and you negotiate an additional $250 off the price (the salesman said was "the lowest he could go" -- yeah right), then you need only one (maybe two) new clients to make that ad work, as opposed to about three.

Many times the money you save on the "extra" advertising expenses you are now NOT PAYING is the actual spread of dollars that keeps you able to spend more on ads, picking up additional clients. Why not keep spending a dollar if you keep getting $1.50 or $1.75 in return? You might stop if your return was .75 cents on the dollar. THAT COULD BE THE DIFFERENCE YOU NEGOTIATED!

Don't forget about bartering, too. Every sales rep, owner of a direct mail company or any other media person you might do business with IS A TAXPAYER, TOO! (It's nice being in a business where everyone has to do (or is supposed to do) the service you provide.)

Anyway, bartering works! We still do it today.

TIP: When you are doing business with a small business owner, they are more likely to go for a "barter deal" than some guy working on commission. (But you never know. ALWAYS throw it out there on the negotiating table and see what happens.)

Probably the most powerful negotiating tool to help you leverage a deal is being able to walk away. "Not having to DO a deal" has great leverage power. If the other person really wants to make the sale, and you don't really "need" to advertise in the media he's selling, you can land a deal you may not want to refuse!

Whenever I'm dealing with an ad rep I never act like I really want what they are offering.

I pay lower prices on advertising because of it. You should, too.

Remember: Never stop asking for a better deal on your ads. The worst they can say is no.

Hold ALL of your advertising media accountable!

Every individual ad you spend your hard earned money on needs to pull its own weight!

Hold it accountable.

Before you spend any more money on advertising, right now, I want you to ...

STOP!

I want you to make a personal commitment before you go any further in your business. I want you to lay down this accountability "law" on yourself and stick to it!

Here it is:

"I will NOT spend money on ANY advertising or marketing ideas, strategies, media, services, etc. that cannot provide viciously accurate, fast measurement of return-on-investment. Period. No exceptions, no excuses."

If you can live by this one commitment in your tax business, each and every tax season, you will quickly mold and shape your company into a lean, mean "money-making" (and profit-building) machine!

Follow through with this one secret, and it'll be worth ALL the time and effort you put into this following my Crash Course Book Strategies.

Strategy #29

The Most Important Part of Any Message

It's the headline, and if you don't get that right…you may as well not even play.

See, the whole point of the headline is to get people INTO the rest of the message. Fail that, and you're sunk.

When I do ad critiques for Members and personal consulting clients, the headline or headlines they use in their ads start out needing improvement. (But these ads are better than the ones that don't have a headline at all.) The headline is THE first part of the ad I look at to see if I can help make it better.

Usually, I'll email back a couple of different examples of headlines that I would suggest using. In a lot of cases (I know from follow up conversations) my client will say that the headline worked and increased the response of the ad.

I'll then say, "What headline did you choose?" And then they will tell me the headline and it's many times a "shortened down version" of what I told them to do.

The client complains the headline was just too long. They thought having a headline three lines long (or more) was just too much. They wanted the standard four or five word headline.

<u>Let's get to this point now rather than later.</u> **The LENGTH of the headline doesn't matter. What matters is response.**

If you get better response from a long headline, then use it. Same with the really short ones. (Sometimes one or two word headlines can be very effective.)

The headline you choose could read either way. Both ways would grab attention:

The Famous *Joe's Tax Service* Guarantee: Fast, Completely Accurate & IRS Protected Tax Returns Prepared In 1 Day Or It's FREE (No Ifs, Ands, Or Buts -- Just Service.)

Or

Taxes Suck.

Length doesn't matter. Just make sure you get attention and pull the reader into the copy. (That's the ONLY job of the headline -- to get you to the next line.)

Don't worry if you think a long headline (or short one) "looks" weird. That's not the point! If it looks weird to you, it might grab attention that much better!

Here's a great tip about headlines: **Don't try and re-invent the wheel!**

There are formulas for headlines that have worked over and over through the years, selling millions and millions of dollars worth of different products and services. Everything from soap to major industrial equipment to tax services to stock options.

And the common denominator with all of these famous promotions is they are all using the same types of formulaic headlines! I'll say this again, too. Don't go out and try to get cute. You do not have to re-invent the wheel here. Just take the same style formula that has worked for some other industry and apply it to the tax business like

I've been doing for years.

Look at these examples of a headline formula, famous "proven" headline and then application to the tax industry:

1. **WARNING:** _____ .

   Warning: Your "Corporate Shield" May Be Made Of Tissue Paper -- 9 Ways You Can Be Held Personally Liable For Your Business' Debts, Losses, or Lawsuits!

   WARNING: Your Tax Return May Have Been Filed INCORRECTLY Last Year! Discover The 5 Most Common Errors Taxpayers Made Not Following The New Tax Laws And How To Keep Uncle Sam From Catching Them!

2. _____ **WAYS TO** _____ .

   99 Ways To Increase New Client Flow!

   17 Ways To Keep The IRS Off Your Back For Good!

3. **IF YOU ARE** _____**, YOU CAN** _____ .

   If You Are A Nondrinker, You Can Save 20% On Life Insurance!

   If You Have A Federal, State, or Local Government Job, You Can Get A 25% Discount Off Your Tax Preparation Fees By Coming Into My Office Before 2/28!

By following formulas that have a proven track record, I'm cutting down on my "unknown variables" that sometimes sabotage a marketing campaign.

The Most Important Part of Any Message
Part 2

When in doubt, start out with your best and most powerful headline and subheads.

In order to make the sale, at some point you have to get the reader's attention with your headline. Now if you never get your prospect's attention, what good is the rest of the ad going to be?

So if you ever have any doubt as to what headline to go with, just think of never getting your prospect's attention and losing money because of it. That should clear your head up pretty quick.

So now, if your life depended on it, what headline would you run?

I heard a famous copywriter once say this is how he decided on the right headline for his sales letters: He imagined a gangster standing behind him as he's at his computer. This mean old greasy guy is his client, and to make sure he does a good job with his sales piece, the gangster has got a gun to his head. If the sales letter doesn't make money, the copywriter gets a big fat hole in the back of his head.

Now that's some pressure! But you see, if you put this kind of pressure on yourself with some extra time, YOUR sales letter -- especially the headline -- will be a lot better. (Maybe we all need to imagine a gangster with a gun behind us as we develop our advertising.)

You can make a better headline by TELEGRAPHING your main and most exciting benefit. Then back it up and add even more selling phrases in your subheads.

Subheads can be just as important as headlines. They should all flow together.

Here are two examples from my old tax business:

FREE Electronic Tax Filing And 1 Day Tax Preparation Service, All Backed By Our "Complete Peace Of Mind" Accuracy GUARANTEE!

Or

[ABC Tax Service] Offers 1 Day (and most times SAME day) Tax Preparation Services And FREE Electronic Filing If We Prepare The Return For Those Who Want An Experienced Tax Professional Helping Them Deal With The NEW Tax Law Changes This Year!

That's for a white collar target market. Here's one for the blue collar target clients:

Instant Tax Loans And FREE Electronic Tax Filing GUARANTEED!

"[ABC Tax Service] Helps You Get Your Refund Loan Check In Your Hands Faster Than You Can Spend It, And You Don't Have To Pay Any Money Up Front!"

(All fees come right out of your refund check,

so don't come to our office with any cash!)

These were some of the best and most powerful reasons to use our tax service as compared to our competition, so we started right out of the gate promoting them!

And guess what? Those pieces got read, they pulled high-response… and the ROI was through the roof.

Strategy #31

Adding Emotional "Zing" ...
Even a Tax Professional Can Do It!

Very few tax business owners add emotion to their promotional material. Most tax practitioners take the pure "logic" approach to crafting their sales message.

Yes, logic backs up your sales argument with facts or reasons to do business with you. But emotional sales copy writing gets the prospect's attention better, gets them involved and "into" your sales message, and then hopefully makes them hot to buy or use your tax services instead of some other tax professional.

It's pretty clear that people BUY from emotion, and then JUSTIFY with logic (after the fact).

I'll tell you the truth right now. If you aren't using EMOTIONAL sales copy to sell your tax services, you're NOT really selling anything! (Don't kid yourself.)

Let me show you the difference between "vanilla, non-emotional" copy and "emotional" copy:

"Use XYZ Tax Service, the experienced tax professional. We will help you fight the IRS, while making sure your tax return is correct and filed on time."

Or

"If you use XYZ Tax Service, you'll be able to sleep at night knowing your taxes are filed correctly, not leaving extra cash for Uncle Sam to suck out of your 'unsuspecting' pockets. You'll rest easy knowing some 'power hungry' IRS agent isn't going to show up on your doorstep demanding to see ALL of your tax records. And your mind will be free of worry knowing if you ever did get some kind of letter from the IRS, you've got a tax professional 'on your side' to handle it."

The difference is obvious. Emotional copy SELLS better, period!

Now the five major emotions you should be using to sell your tax services better are:

1) Fear
2) Guilt
3) Pride
4) Greed (Desire) and
5) Love

Now, another word about using this stuff—it's NOT "manipulative"…it's where people (your clients) actually "live." If you don't speak to these realities, you're not actually connecting with your prospects. We are much more emotions-driven than we realize!

Probably the one that I like to use the most because we are in the tax business is fear.

The fear emotion sells well in our industry because we have a built-in "fear factor" called the IRS! Almost everyone you talk to has heard some "awful" story of how the IRS did something bad to an innocent taxpayer, so there's some level of fear of the IRS.

In many cases, people feel the hair on the back of their neck stick up when you start talking about the IRS and auditing tax returns or IRS agents going through their personal finances.

Whether this is justified or not, the perception is THE IRS IS

THE BAD GUY, SO YOU BETTER FILE YOUR TAXES CORRECTLY AND ON TIME!

We as tax business owners have to use this built in advantage we have in our industry!

You can "trigger" many emotions in other people by talking about the subject of taxes in an EMOTIONAL way. Everyone has certain "hot buttons" that cause them to "act" or take action in a way that brings them closer to buying or using a service.

By the way, having a "built in deadline" for people to use our services also helps the emotional copy to sell better.

Here's How To Use "Fear of Pain (or Loss)"

Yes, "fear of pain" does sell the best. People tend to spend a lot of time, money and energy avoiding pain. The smart marketer understands this and is willing to "peel back a scab and rub salt in it" to motivate someone to action.

A savvy tax business owner who understands the emotional side of getting taxpayers to use their tax services knows using the "fear of pain" to his or her advantage (every place they can) will help increase the effectiveness of their marketing.

The bottom line: If you can whip up this insecurity and fear, you will sell more.

Now don't get me wrong. You want to sell benefits, too! What I'm saying is you need to do BOTH with a little more of the weight leaning on the "fear of pain" side.

You see, once you make taxpayers feel miserable about their current tax situation, you can then liberate them by being the best solution to their tax problems (or POTENTIAL problems).

That's why you need to implement both FEAR and BENEFIT selling, spending more time in the beginning scaring them to death and then selling them on you being the best solution to their possible problems. (Remember the selling formula: Problem, Agitate, Solution.)

<u>What is PAINFUL (or at least feared as painful) to your target market?</u>

How about an IRS agent walking into your business?
Example:

> "... the last thing you need is to make a simple mistake on your tax return that triggers an IRS 'red flag' and the next thing you know you've got some pesky IRS agent coming into your office on a Monday morning wanting to see your records."

How about an IRS audit of your personal tax return?
Example:

> "... regular ol' folks that keep paying more than they are supposed to in taxes, believing it will 'shield' them from ever getting one of those nasty IRS letters in the mail, are in denial. IRS audits are real and can be very painful, costly, time-consuming, and even embarrassing!"

So the main question going through your head right now should be, "What is my target market's biggest fear or frustration as it relates to taxes?"

When you start getting a handle on what makes your target market "tick" and understanding what their main "hot buttons" are, I guarantee somewhere in the mix you'll be able to point to some fear or "possibility of pain" they want to avoid as being a key factor in what actually motivates them to action.

It might be a phone call. It might be a person showing up at your office unannounced one day. But what got that prospect to USE YOU instead of someone else can be traced back to you helping them avoid the possibility of pain.

And as Barretta used to say, "You can take that one to the bank!"

Important. Keep some of the "logical" stuff you already have in your ads because you ultimately need both to complete the sales message. I'm just saying add more emotional copy (even on the heavy side) because that's what helps make the phone ring!

Strategy #32

Passion and Clarity—Together!

Remember, the number one marketing sin is being boring! So one of the fastest ways to make your ads and promotional pieces better is to add PASSION and DRAMA to your sales copy. But you have to do this with CLARITY as well (I'll get to that second, after passion).

I guess I should ask you now: Are you passionate about your work? Do you get excited helping people solve their tax problems? Do you get a rush out of doing something for someone that they couldn't do and then having them PAY you for it?

Well, that's what you are doing when you prepare tax returns for a living. (And, if you can't get excited about what you do for a living, do something that does get you excited!)

The excitement should come out in your ads and in all of your promotional material. When you are excited about what you are doing, other people (like your clients) will get excited, too.

What? You say people will get excited about taxes? No, people will get excited that they are doing business with a tax practitioner that loves what he or she does. And if they see you are really "into it," then they will feel more comfortable with you taking care of their tax situation.

Passion helps get your prospects' attention and it'll help keep it. And when in doubt, throw a little DRAMA in there to keep the ball rolling! The famous mystery writer, Dashiell Hammet, once said, "When in doubt, have someone come crashing through the door with a gun."

This is very true in a mystery novel, but even more important for your advertising and sales copy.

Once you get someone's attention, it's hard to always keep it. Injecting the added passion and drama will increase your readership, which will translate to more sales in the end. One way I do this is add a warning phrase right in the middle of my ad copy.

The prospect would be reading along and then I'd say,

"WARNING: [ABC Tax Service] won't be responsible for spending the money you're gonna save by using us instead of some national tax franchise!"

It's my way of "crashing through the door with a gun" and keeping the reader interested in my "story" or my sales message.

You've got your own passions and you can come up with your own drama to make your advertising come alive, so use them.

Because your competition will still be promoting "vanilla" or boring ads, the passion and drama in your marketing will stand out even more!

Clarity Too...

One huge flaw that I see in new "eager beaver" tax business owners learning the skill of marketing is they try to be too "cute" with their message.

They see these big time brand name companies using MASS MEDIA to "blanket" every corner on the earth with their marketing message. They see the TV ads, the internet ads, the full page glossy magazine ads, the multi page ads in USA Today, and those ads are all "slogany" and kind of "cutesy" sounding. (For instance, think about Budweiser commercials. I rest my case.)

So if huge advertising agencies getting paid millions of dollars to produce ads with a message, you sort of have to figure out what they are saying because they are being cute. Or you sometimes have to look hard to even see WHO the advertiser is or what they are even advertising when you're reading and viewing an ad.

Why is that? Many reasons, but here are the main ones: First of all, "Madison Ave." ad agencies have no clue how to really market anything! (By that I mean measuring ad expense to actual sales and turning a profit.) These agencies want to do everything possible NOT to measure the results so the client won't be able to see how much money they are actually flushing down the toilet every month.

They do this (and get away with murder) by selling to the client on the importance of "brand awareness" or "getting their name out there," and over a period of time the product or service will "sell itself." (These are some of the biggest lies in marketing.)

Second, by NOT having the message clear or easily understandable, the ad is "cool" or "hip" and has a chance to win some stupid advertising award at the end of the year.   But the only award you ad should win is a financial one. DID IT MAKE MONEY? Did your marketing investment "RE-ward" you with a profit?

These large worldwide companies can afford to lose millions each year building "brand awareness," but you and I can't! That's why you DON'T MODEL YOUR ADVERTISING MESSAGE AFTER THESE RIDICULOUS ADS!

For this reason, you should concentrate on making your message clear, readable, and easy to understand. That means from the headline, all the way through your whole sales message. If you have a son or daughter in middle school, you should get them to read over EVERY piece of marketing material you've got! If they can read and understand it, you are on the right track!

NEVER OVER-ESTIMATE THE INTELLIGENCE OF YOUR TARGET MARKET.

If your target market is high-income executives, then you should be writing at about a sixth grade level. If you don't have a middle-schooler in your house to read over your sales copy, go watch four or five old episodes of "The Simpsons" on your local Fox channel. Pay attention to HOMER SIMPSON. Watch, listen, and learn from everything he does, says, or thinks.

Now go change your sales material so he'd clearly and easily understand your message.

Why? Because in "reality," Homer Simpson is all of our target market. Even the "high end" client. (You think I'm wrong? YOU'RE reading this right? Well, I "sold" you using Homer-Talk!)

If Homer gets it...they will too.

Getting The Two Main "Types" Of Readers

Since one of the main goals of your advertising will be clarity and being easily understood, you'll need to make sure you're doing this for as many people as you can at the same time.

You see, people are different. Some like to skim and just get the "big picture," while others like diving in and catching all the details. The skimmers tend to be IMPULSIVE people, while the detailed folks are the ANALYTICAL ones. Both are good prospects, you just need to sell them in a different way.

Let's compare "analytical" vs. "impulsive."

ANALYTICAL likes:	**IMPULSIVE prefers:**
Lot of sales copy	A telegraphed offer
Facts, figures and stats	The bottom line
Logical case	An emotional appeal
Charts and graphs	Pictures or photos
The more info, the better	Skimming when possible
Credible testimonials	Celebrity testimonials

Are you starting to get the picture? (I bet you can tell right away which one you are.)

So now we have to figure out how to you write and sell to BOTH kinds of prospects. And the best way is to use the "double readership path" technique.

When you use this technique, you are giving the prospect (no matter whether analytical or impulsive) what they WANT! So when the prospect opens your letter and reads your headline, what do they do next?

The analytical one will tend to start from the first sentence and begin reading your letter without skipping ahead. The impulsive person will glance down and catch your first SUBHEADING and skim to the next, maybe even turning to the end to read the P.S. or see the "offer," but mainly getting the gist of your letter through subheads, bullet points, photo captions, etc.

What are some other "tricks" to use to get the impulsive person back into your sales copy? You can underline text, boldface main words, box a paragraph, use different type styles, maybe a different color ink or even writing margin notes off to the side of the page.

The combination of a long, detailed logical copy coupled with the emotional appeals of added subheads, extra P.S. points etc. will sell more because you are "appealing" to both groups of people.

Something to remember: Your "impulsive prospect" should be able to catch and understand your whole sales message by just reading your headlines, subheadings, bullet points, P.S. and other mail-skimming items, even if they NEVER went back into your letter and read all the details about your offer and/or tax services.

That's important because it happens more than you think!

Strategy #34

Insider Message Tricks

Repeat yourself.

Have you ever heard the nutritionists say, "Strive for Five?" They are trying to encourage people to eat at least five fruits and vegetables each day. Well, I've got another one for you.

STRIVE FOR SEVEN! That means: **Try and state your main offer or your most compelling benefit for using your tax services seven times on any given promotion.** Obviously, advertising space will affect this, but you know what the goal is.

Tax business owners wonder, "How in the heck can I state my offer seven times without sounding like a bumbling idiot?" Well, here's how.

Make a straightforward statement or promise in the beginning of your ad. Incorporate the same idea into your guarantee. Add a "YES" and then state your guarantee in the copy of your response form. Then you can have a satisfied client basically say the same thing in a testimonial. You could tell a story backing up this same promise or guarantee. Add a few bullet points building up the specific benefits of this same offer. And then finally say it in so many words in your P.S. at the end.

That's how you can effectively repeat yourself seven times and not sound like a fool.

Why go to all of this trouble? Now you know what my answer is ALWAYS going to be to a question like that: INCREASED SALES!

Repetition is REQUIRED for impact. If you want to be an effective seller of your services, you are going to have to tell them the offer or main benefit, tell them again, and then finally tell them some more!

If you've read or studied anything about what I teach on the subject of length, you've heard me say, "The more you tell, the more you sell!"

This is very true. But many people get "caught up" in the idea that long sales copy doesn't get read. NOT TRUE if your message in your sales letter is being read by the right targeted prospect. As long as you're not being boring, your sales letter can be over 100 pages! (If it takes that long to tell your WHOLE SALES STORY, then that's what you have to do.)

The big marketing myth among those NOT in the know is "keep your sales letters short and sweet so your prospects will read them."

But the REAL truth is if you've done a good job up front (like you are supposed to) at selecting your market, the longer your sales letter, THE BETTER!

I'm a personal believer that long sales copy outsells short, hands down. That doesn't mean that short copy can't sell because there are plenty of examples where it does just fine.

My point is, in order to be effective in your sales pitch, you have to use internal repetition throughout your sales copy. To do so means you will be writing more copy and having a longer sales letter.

That's OK! Don't be afraid of a "longer" sales pitch in writing. I'll bet if you test the two ways (long vs. short), you'll find out for yourself what I always keep saying: "The more you tell, the more you sell!"

Wimpy Messages

Boy, I see a lot of "wimpy" advertising out there in the tax industry! In most cases the tax professional is basically advertising a "glorified" business card look (name, company, contact info, and slogan).

If you are going to be serious about getting some more business from your advertising, then you need to start giving good reasons for people to use you and then ASK THEM TO DO SO!

Why just do business card type ads, to "get your name out there?" (Out where? What is it doing? How is it helping you?)

Give me specific examples and show me where advertising like this is beneficial. You can't, so stop doing this kind of WASTEFUL advertising! And start being BOLD by making your target clients powerful, specific, irresistible offers, and then call them to ask immediately! (That's NOT wimpy advertising. That's REAL marketing!)

Hopefully you've heard of Zig Ziglar. He was one of the most famous sales trainers in the world.

Zig has many quotes that I like, but this one fits the topic we're discussing to a tee: "Are you a professional salesman, or a professional visitor?"

Now let's take his question and apply it to our industry: "<u>Are you really selling your tax services, or do just a lot of people in your town know you are in the tax business?</u>"

There's a difference between "making the sale" and making some acquaintances.

If you have MORE people coming up to you on the street saying they saw your ads instead of saying, "Can I come by your office today or do I need to make an appointment for you to prepare my taxes?" you've got a problem.

You need to work on your "call to action" ASAP! Here are four specific things you can do to change your advertising or update your current response device to increase your response:

1. Tell your client exactly WHAT you want them to do
2. Tell your client exactly HOW you want them to do it

3. Tell your client exactly WHEN you want them to do it

And finally,

    4. GIVE THEM A CLEAR INCENTIVE TO DO IT AS YOU HAVE REQUESTED IN #1 THROUGH #3!

If you want to increase your current response (AND WANT TO STOP BEING A WIMPY ADVERTISER), then these are NON-negotiable!

Strategy #35

A Solid Structure For A "Call To Action"

Here's the major difference between TRADITIONAL media advertising and DIRECT RESPONSE (measuring) advertising: one calls the prospect to action and asks for the order, and the other one doesn't.

When you market your tax business like I'm teaching you to, you can't afford to be "skirting around" the real issue.

The real issue is:

The reason this ad is front of you, Mr. Prospect, IS ...

> "I feel I have the best 'doggone' tax business in the city, and the bottom line is you would be MUCH better off letting me help you file your taxes this year compared to anything else you could do. And I'm even willing to prove it to you by guaranteeing 'this,' and you have my word on 'that' and as an extra bonus I want you to have _____ for coming into my office before I get swamped in April"

This kind of message gets results. (We will not be following "Madison Ave." Ad Agencies as our model for success!)

But if I could give you one solid "action structure" to model, it'd be this one.

At the end of your sales letter or ad try adding the following list of ideas as helpful closes:

1) Summarize the offer
2) Show Value - Price - Discount - Net Cost
3) Include the guarantee
4) Provide payment options
5) Add bonus

And remember, since we are talking about a short "selling cycle" (tax season), you can come up with a variety of ideas for prospects to take IMMEDIATE action:

A) **Limited Number Available** -- (Ex. My staff and I can only prepare a limited number of more NEW tax returns this tax season before the IRS April 15th deadline.)

B) **Most Will Buy** -- (Ex. Once they see our ad and find out we specialize in your kind of tax situation, most people in your profession call us and set an appointment immediately. The ones that don't, well, there are only 24 hours in a day, and we can't take everyone as a new client.)

C) **Discounts / Bonus Gift(s) Tied To Immediate Response** -- (Ex. To encourage you to respond quickly, I've made arrangements to give the first 25 new clients that call a new "X" worth over $25! I only have this limited number, so if you're the 26th person to call our office, I'm sorry.)

Following these "call to action" formulas EVERY TIME will help you close more sales and increase your profitability of your overall business!

TIP: The better the "reasons" for immediate response and the better the bonus gifts you end up offering, THE BETTER YOUR MARKETING WILL WORK!

Closing the Deal — In An Ad

NEGATIVE emotions work even better than selling the benefits of your tax service.

As you are developing and using certain proven "closing" techniques, always have the client's **"fear of loss"** thoughts running around in the back of your head. As you write your promotions, you should never allow the potential targeted prospect's thoughts to stray too far from yours.

As we talked about already, you want to do everything in your power to get the client to commit to you and your tax service as early in the tax season as humanly possible. Setting up a variety of "early bird specials" is always a good idea.

(Side Note: Early Bird Specials I've tried in the past with deadline dates on February 1st or before never seemed to pan out too well. My guess has something to do with W-2s and other tax related documents not getting to my potential markets in a timely manner. Even with new software programs and companies getting all their tax documents out earlier and earlier, to be on the safe side, use dates in the middle of February as the earliest "special offer" datelines for your clients.)

Expiration dates or "deadline" dates are a MUST in all your ads! If you don't have one of these dates tied to your offer, you're NOT using people's natural "fear of loss by delay" to your advantage.

Is the "fear of loss" that powerful? In some people it really is a motivating factor. But these deadlines or expiration dates do more than just motivate out of fear of not getting something other people are going to get, leaving them out.

It has to do with your prospect putting your offer aside and "dealing with it later." That is dangerous! The more your target market puts off your offers, the more sales you'll lose.

You know the deal. You and I do the same thing. We read an ad and think to ourselves we'd sure like to buy this or that. We put the newspaper down, or we say we'll come back to the magazine later, and "whoops," the sale is gone forever.

It's not like we intentionally put the ad aside. We really were interested in buying whatever it was. But the busy life goes on, and the ad is either forgotten about, or if we do come back to it, we don't have the same "buying" emotions we did the first time around.

(This happens all across America every day. If there was some way you could measure it, I'd be willing to bet you there are billions of lost orders going on every day.)

Using the "P.S."

As you close the deal in your letters, or ads, it's ALWAYS a good idea to end with a signature line from YOU the business owner. And when you do so, you can take advantage of the SECOND most-read item of any letter -- the "P.S.".

Many times the P.S. is not considered as the powerful selling tool it really is. How do I know that? Because many tax business owners never use a P.S. in their sales letters, and if they do, it's not used to "sell" anything. (The answer to "When should I use a P.S?" is EVERY TIME.)

Did you know studies show that, after the headline, **the P.S. has the second highest readership of everything in your sales letter.** That's right, second! Pretty good for being at the end of a sales letter.

What's the reason? I'm not sure, but here's my guess. The prospect either reads your letter from cover to cover or he reads the headline and tries to decide if going any further is worth his time. I think he turns to the end to try and find out the "punch line," and BOOM there's your P.S.!

Now here's your next big chance (maybe your last) to get the prospect into your sales letter.

You can either write a waste of a P.S. and say something cute, or you can really make it a solid sales part of your overall letter with a message that'll get the reader to go back to the beginning of the copy and start reading.

OK, how do you use a P.S.? In my experience you can go two or three different routes. First, you can summarize your main offer all over again in your P.S. It works, especially for those "jumpers" that go to the end of your letter so impatiently.

Second, you can emphasize THE most important benefit to the reader. Obviously this kind of P.S. would help get that prospect back into the "body" of your letter.

And third, you can do what I do the most and that's write multiple P.S.'s! I've found that two can be better than one, and three can be more effective than two. I'll summarize the whole offer with one, include the MOST POWERFUL BENEFIT in the second P.S., and in the final P.S.

I'll emphasize one of the prospect's main fears, and/or remind them about a deadline date (to keep the "fear of loss" in the front of their mind as they consider my offer).

To make your P.S.'s stand out even more, try these little tricks of the trade:

- vary the type style and/or point size
- use all caps if one of your P.S.'s is short
- add a color to one of them
- hand write the last P.S.

- "block screen" the background of a P.S.
- in your handwriting, scribble up the side of the letter (like you ran out of room)

Make sure you add a postscript to all of your letters from now on. Thanks.

P.S. Here's a P.S. to end this strategy on using postscripts.

:--)

Tweaking Messages That Work

Once you've found an ad or a sales letter that's working for you (or you've got a "control" to test from) try adding a "grabber" to your sales piece to see if you can boost response!

A "control" means you have tested a specific message, to a specific market, using a specific media, and now you are getting steady and predictable results every time you advertise.

When you have a few "systematic" ads running, you want to always try to see if you can beat your current "control" or the "predictable numbers" you usually get when you run this particular promotion. "Grabbers" are the first place to test if you are using some kind of sales letter.

An example of an effective grabber would be a real $1 bill. Sending real cash in the mail gets people's attention! Paperclipping it to the top of your sales letter and making some reference to it in your headline or subhead should give your letter a "boost" because more people will take the time to read this important letter that's been mailed with cash in it!

Another solid grabber I use often is a fake "million dollar" bill. It can be just as effective as a real dollar bill because people haven't seen this before, and the cost is much cheaper per unit (.15 cents). If the reader's attention is grabbed, then the grabber has done its job. Your solid sales letter will do the rest.

Using "money" as a grabber in the tax business is easy. But how about some other options? Check these out!

- Tylenol (or little Alka Seltzer packets)

  Idea: "With all the new tax laws this year, you probably have a headache just thinking about your tax situation. Your best bet is to take these two tablets, read my letter, and call me in the morning."

- Dice

  Idea: "Don't gamble on filing your taxes incorrectly this year. Our tax return accuracy guarantee takes all the risk! (Don't roll the dice and 'crap out' with Uncle Sam just sitting there waiting for you to make a mistake!)"

- Pistol Key Chain

  Idea: "If you pass up this opportunity (never offered before by another tax business in this area) you'll probably want to shoot yourself!"

The sky's the limit on ideas you can come up with. I'd get my hands on some of these companies that have "close out" specials on stuff like this. You can get these little grabbers for cheap, and they have the potential to boost your response and increase your bottom line!

Here's the name of a "close out" distributor I've used in the past.

3 D Mail

http://3dmailresults.com/

And if you want to try some **fake Million Dollar bills**, just Google it. (lots of inexpensive options to choose from)

Mail a "Selling Package"…not just an Ad

Many tax professionals get their hands on a "mailing list" of (hopefully) hot prospects and write their best sales letter ever and mail it as fast as they can.

Hey, I like the enthusiasm, but don't go into battle with one arm tied behind your back! If you are ONLY mailing one sales letter, you are limiting your weapons to getting effective response rates which go a long way to improving your take home pay for the year.

What else should you send, you ask? Well, to increase your response you can always add an attention grabber to the top of your sales letter -- a response device of some sort with your main offer and contact information.

A coupon is always a good idea (more about those in a minute). Don't be afraid to add a few extra sheets of paper of only testimonials (ie. "preponderance of proof"). How about a return envelope? (Test adding postage or not.) Or try a picture of yourself and a listing of all the reasons people have trusted you to help them with their taxes over the last "___" years.

Add a cover letter or a "lift note" explaining why this offer is so great or why it is so "time sensitive"(not only because April 15th is coming, but because I can only make this offer for a limited time because there is only one of me, etc.)

You see, there are many different things you can test that can bring high response rates to your current mailing. Don't just send one sales letter and hope that it would work.

Don't get me wrong, it might work. The problem is it most likely won't, and if it did, it would've worked EVEN BETTER if you'd tried any of these other "sales pieces" and made a SELLING PACKAGE!

A different combination of selling ingredients will work with different markets. Test now, and keep testing often! You'll have fun figuring out which combination works best with each market you target.

<u>One final note about coupons</u>: I've found making a coupon look a

little "snazzier" helps response. A dotted line works better than a regular border (the thicker the better). Don't be afraid to use coupons with any kind of target market (even high-end clients). Everyone likes the idea of getting a deal. Also, add to your sales material that you accept "competitor's coupons." I was surprised how well this little line worked in one of our offices. Try it in your town.

Free Recorded Messages

Remember, almost everyone walking around these days is SKEPTICAL. Every large and small company imaginable is trying to promise them the world, and they get tired of being bombarded with the constant pressure of thousands of sales messages hitting their brains every day!

How do you break through the clutter? How do you come across as not being a "pushy salesman?" How can you get your sales message heard when your prospect actually takes the time to listen to it?

All of these questions and more can be answered by using three little words at the end of your ad (or in your contact information): "FREE RECORDED MESSAGE." If you are "selling" your prospect on making a phone call and listening to a "robot" tell them the things they want to know, there's no sales pressure!

The prospect can learn more at their own speed. They let their guard down because they know they won't have to be talking to a "live" person. Skepticism is reduced because the prospect controls whether they want to hear more or not.

Having a "no extra cost" option for your prospect gives them a chance to learn more about you and your services, plus at the same time they are actually qualifying themselves as a good or bad prospect depending on what they decide to do.

If they like what they hear, they can leave their name and address to get some follow up information mailed to them. If they don't, they hang up. That means you probably didn't want to spend money pursuing them as a client anyway. They "weeded" themselves out of your selling cycle for you. That's good!

Your "leads" from one ad can double by just adding these three words to your promotion!
I recommend using ATG Technologies for recorded message services.

www.PatLive.com

The "Acres of Diamonds" Theory

I've found through working with tax professionals in the tax industry that they tend to be interested in how other tax business owners advertise and promote their tax businesses to the public.

They see the "greener pastures" in their competition's advertising and they have a tendency to want to follow in their promotional footsteps.

Now, if the other tax business really is promoting and advertising in a way that is truly effective, by all means take a hard look at what they are doing. But in most cases, the "greener pasture phenomenon" is what's actually going on; that is, you just THINK the other tax business owner's EXTERNAL advertising is probably the better way to go, so you give it a try.

This is a BAD approach to promoting YOUR tax office!

Why do I say that?

Because you and most every other tax business owner on this planet has "hidden treasures" sitting right under your nose in your own client base!

You see, one of the greatest marketing secrets of all time is to tap into "the unmined gold" which exists in your client list.

There are "acres of diamonds" in EVERY tax business' database right now. And the quicker you get this through your head and understand the potential profit sitting at your fingertips, the better! You've neglected to mine this profit center in the past. Now I want to help you SEE "with fresh eyes" the riches in your own clients' folders!

I want to share a quick example showing you the importance of this marketing strategy and how many other businesses "miss it" when they don't target their clients as much as they should.

Jay Abraham, a famous marketing consultant, has made a very nice living over the years consulting in this "niche" area alone. He puts on large seminars on the west coast at $25,000 a head revealing the "acres of diamonds" approach. The main theme of the whole seminar is "exploiting the under-valued, neglected asset" of each company in the room --their client lists!

(Business owners are happy to pay the $25,000 because once they understand what they've been missing, they will make far more money in the future.)

You don't need to go to this "high priced" seminar to learn this. I'm going to teach you everything you need to know right now in the next step or two.

The Lifetime Value of Your Client Dictates Your Marketing Plan

What is getting a new client worth to you? Would you spend $20 to get a new client? How about spending $50 to get a new client? Suppose you are averaging about $400 per return and you had a guy on the street come up to you and say, "I'll bring you five new clients a day for thirty days if you will give me $300 a piece for each of them."

Would you give someone $300 bucks for every new client they brought you so you could then turn around and net an additional $100 on the deal the next day? (Well, I should hope so.) That's like saying, "Hey buddy, you bring me two $100 bills, and I'll give you one of those $100 bills back, and let's do it at least ten times a day for the next month!"

This sounds like an easy question to answer, but I run into tax business owners all the time who refuse to give out money for referrals. (Greed? Stupidity?) Look, I know people are going to refer your tax business to other people whether you reward someone with cash or not. That's not the point.

The BIGGER ISSUE is understanding what one particular client is worth to you over the "lifetime" he or she does business with your tax service!

You see, if you had enough money to "bankroll" yourself for a couple of tax seasons and not take any money out of the business, you could afford to "BUY" more market share and broaden your client base to be the most dominant tax business in your area.

What do I mean by "buying" clients? Well, if you understand the LIFETIME VALUE of your typical client, you can estimate the revenue he or she will generate over the next five or ten years.

You could go through your database right now and see on average how long a typical client continues to return and do business with you. (Three years, six years, maybe more.) Let's say, after you average all your clients from the last ten years, considering those that stay only one year, you estimate that your typical clients will stick with you about five years. (That's five years multiplied by $400 per return, or a $2,000 lifetime value!)

Now let's go back to the example of the man on the street. It's the next tax season and you now have a better understanding of your clients' lifetime value. Let's say he comes up to you and says, I can bring you ten new clients per day for a month; are you interested in giving me $500 apiece for each of them? (Your fees staying the same.) Knowing what you know now, would you sacrifice some (or maybe all) of this year's tax season profits and put it towards "bank rolling" 300 new clients into your business?

How you answer this question will determine your overall marketing strategy.

Stimulating Word of Mouth and Referrals

<u>Definition of a Referral:</u> Clients that do business with you as a result of the satisfaction of your current or previous clients. They can be first, second, third, or more generation. (They may come from someone who told someone, who told someone ... etc.)

<u>Purpose of Referrals:</u> To increase your business without the cost of marketing or advertising. (Or increase client acquisition at a much lower cost than normal external advertising means.)

With this said, let me point out there is no better new client that will come into your tax business than one referred by a happy client. The referred client comes into your office with less price resistance, less skepticism, and more receptivity overall. (By the way, if you do a good job, they tend to refer even more of THEIR friends, co-workers, etc.)

Now the "EAR" formula is a simple way for you to use referrals to increase your ongoing tax business.

E.A.R. stands for EARN, ASK and REWARD. Every tax business should be doing "some" part of the "EAR" formula as a natural extension of their normal business practices.

If you are good at what you do (and you should be), you will naturally "earn" more business because your clients WILL talk positively about you. By taking care of your clients, you will **EARN** the right to move to the next part of the formula.

Yes, if you are GOOD (hopefully you're GREAT) at preparing taxes and making your clients feel taken care of, then you should have NO problem **"ASKING" for referrals!**

I don't know why so many people get "hung up" on this point. It may be a self esteem issue or just a low self confidence problem, but you're going to have to get over this "bump in the road" real quick!

Not being confident in your abilities to do "what you do" for a living needs to be resolved. That's something I can't help you with.

And finally, the "R" stands for RECOGNIZE or REWARD. If you have gone this far to EARN your client's approval, and you've been bold enough to ASK for referrals, then you should finish the race by **REWARDING your clients for doing what you asked them to do in the first place!**

(Some tax business owners just don't like rewarding or recognizing their clients for referring their friends, neighbors, etc. I think there must be some pride or greed issues going on deep down, but that's for them to deal with.)

Here's a quick story that illustrates how your clients will respond to being rewarded for their "good behavior." (I got this from a guy in a "Marketing Mastermind Group".)

> *"A guy rows his little boat out to the middle of a lake for a relaxing day of fishing. Up over the side of the boat comes a huge green snake with a half-swallowed frog sticking out of his mouth. Feeling for the frog, the fisherman whacks the snake with the oar; the snake spits out the frog; and the frog's life is spared -- and that makes the guy feel good. But he also knows he has just deprived the snake of his mid-day meal -- and that makes him feel bad. Having no food for him, he gives the snake a swig out of his bottle of bourbon, and the snake swims away happy. Two minutes later the snake swims back with two frogs in his mouth."*

You'd be surprised what your clients will do when you offer them a little reward or recognition!

How to use the "EAR Formula" specifically to increase your sales

Let's start off with EARN first. How can you be so good at offering tax services that you "earn" word of mouth business? (This may be one of your "ultimate secret marketing" weapons.)

The answer is simple but hard to "really" implement on a consistent basis. The simple answer is EXCELLENCE. That's right, your office should "ooze" with the smell of excellent service! I can walk into one of our tax offices during the peak of tax season and see this "excellence" taking place. It makes my heart feel good: All the time and effort and work that went into developing a system that runs like a top.

Employees are smiling, enjoying the "fast pace" of all the business. Clients are getting taken care of fast and efficiently. You can just look at them and tell they are happy. The phone is being answered properly and new clients are being "sold" with every other ring. It's an excellent environment to be in.

Does it always run that smoothly? (I wish.) If you can get an "environment of excellence" 85% to 90% of the time you're way ahead of the game! We're all human and we all make mistakes. And you know what, life "just happens" sometimes and there's not a lot we can do about it. An employee doesn't show up for a shift, you get two "problem" clients in a row and your "attitude" is temporarily bruised, and at the same time a computer breaks down.

Again, that's life! Roll with it and chalk it up to the 10% or 15% you just can't control.

Now what are some of the best times to ASK for referrals? (We ask before, during and after the tax return has been prepared.) Why so many times? (Well, why not?)

Our clients got TWO letters at the beginning of tax season (whether they have come in already or not.) They were both "referral pitches" asking existing clients to tell their friends about us.

When clients came in our lobby during tax season we had brochures and fliers promoting our "Refer-A-Friend" plan. When a tax preparer took a client back and sat down with them to prepare their return on the computer, an "inquiry" or "soft sell" was made talking about the referral program. When the client's return was completed, he or she received a brochure or flier (with referral slips to give to their friends) before leaving. When they came back to pick up their refund check or to get the copies of their completed return, we gave them more referral slips and "talked up" the reward benefits.

We even give Free Gifts to our clients as a "good will" gesture to help stimulate more Word Of Mouth. (WOM) More about that in a minute.

Finally, we'd send letters thanking clients for their business and ASKING for referrals AGAIN! If they had already referred someone, we gave them their reward and thanked them some more.

This is called a referral "funnel", and it's critical.

Speaking of REWARDS, we said thank you with CASH! People love getting cash sent to them in the mail! $10 bucks, a $20 bill or a handful of $2 bills ... because no one ever does it! It's a great way to spread even more "positive talk" about your tax business. If clients kept referring more people, once they got to a certain level we gave them even more "bonus" money! You can be as creative as you want!

The point is to recognize and reward behavior that adds more money to your pocket!

I like to think of our referral plan as a way of hiring thousands of salespeople to go out and "sell" other people on using our tax services. If they "make a sale" they get something like a commission check. (But in our case, it was actually just a thank you letter and cash. It works well enough.)

Another important note to sending cash in the mail: <u>SEND OUT YOUR THANK YOU NOTE WITH THE CASH ASAP</u>! (DON'T

DELAY ON THIS. IT WILL COST YOU MOMENTUM AND LOST SALES!)

This sounds pretty easy, right? So why do so many tax business owners NOT have effective referral promotions? Well, it all boils down to two main reasons: **PRIORITY and ACCOUNTABILITY.**

You see, "knowing" and "doing" are two different balls of wax!

It has been my experience that everyone in the tax business KNOWS that referrals, combined with business from word of mouth are the main sources for new clients during any given tax season. (Every tax business owner gets them.)

The key I've found is NOT EVERY TAX BUSINESS OWNER MAKES GETTING MORE REFERRALS A PRIORITY!

They know if they do a good job people will talk well about them. They know if they ask their clients for some referrals, they get some extra people coming to their office. And finally, they know if they give some extra incentive, more people will be willing tell their friends about their tax business.

"KNOWING" is not the problem! Set an example as the owner of the business (following the EAR Formula yourself) and make sure your staff is "crystal clear" on the fact that getting referrals in your office WILL be a mandatory part of their job description!
But how do you implement it properly? I mean, how do you make this whole thing happen like it's supposed to?

An ACCOUNTABILITY system is the sure fire way to make implementation "stick."

If you are holding yourself and your staff accountable to **ASKING EVERY CLIENT THAT WALKS THROUGH YOUR DOOR TO PLEASE CONSIDER REFERRING OTHERS TO YOUR TAX BUSINESS** (AND HANDING THEM AN INCENTIVE COUPON SLIP), that will be one way to do it.

Another way would be to set a goal to mail a certain number of letters per week to your clients (or even to your friends or neighbors that are not clients) and ask them to send new clients your way.

You could make this a contest for everyone in your office. They can mail a certain number of people per week that they know (with the business paying for the mailing, of course.) You get everything up on a board in the back of your office or in a break room with some kind of chart tracking "how everyone is doing."

This helps make it fun, it gets other people more excited because they will be naturally competitive about it, but most of all, you get to hold EVERYONE accountable at the same time.

You can have multiple contests. Track the number of contacts each employee has with a client compared to the number of referral slips they have handed out. You can track a different number of referral slips given to other people inside or outside your office.

We actually had one employee get so excited about handing out referral coupons that she just walked around a shopping center handing out referral slips to people WHO WERE NOT EVEN OUR CLIENTS. She won the contest in her office and it was because she had almost fifteen other people in that town walking around giving our referral slips to THEIR friends, and they weren't even in our client base! (Of course we sent them the cash in the mail. I don't care WHO refers someone, as long as we get new paying clients!)

Offer steak dinners at the end of each month of the tax season for the most new client referrals coming from your employees' hard work. Hey, offer them more cash if they want it, just like you're giving your clients.

Track whatever way you want. Just make sure it is a priority and you are holding the whole program accountable.

The main thing to remember is: Nike. (Just do it.)

Strategy #40

Recognizing and Rewarding Your Clients

Find your "CHAMPION" CLIENTS and treat them like kings!

We all have heard of the "80/20 Rule." It applies to many situations. In this case, I'm applying it to referrals and where most of them come from.

Yes, **80% of your referrals will come from 20% of your clients.** Since this is true, you should concentrate 80% of your time finding out who is most likely to be in that 20% group and then pour gasoline on that word of mouth "wild fire!"

If you knew ahead of time which 20% of your client base would refer 80% of the new clients to you, I'd say spend ALL of your time "working" that group of clients. Since you have to find out, that means, initially, you have to talk to everyone.

Some people will be more receptive than others. Other people will send you two or three clients right off the bat. These clients have a good chance of getting in your 20% group! Set these folks' names aside and mail out multiple more mailings to them, giving them added incentive bonuses for even more people they send your way.

Now in that 20% group, you will have a few "special" clients. They are what I call CHAMPION clients. These people absolutely love you! They think you can walk on water almost anytime you want. Every tax business has clients like this in their database. If they don't come out and tell you how great they think you are, watch for "signs" that they are telling everyone else!

A few years back, I had a client come up to me in the lobby of our office and stop me and say, "Do you see all of these people in here? I told them to come down and see you guys." I looked around and about twelve people in the room nodded their heads, indicating that this was true. I thanked him for saying nice things about us and I went on my way.

About two days later I saw the same guy in our lobby. I asked him how he was doing and if he was still having his taxes prepared. He said no, but he was just at the office again showing some of his neighbors how to find the place. He then proceeded to call them out by name, pointing to each one. That day there were seven more people waiting in the lobby he had brought to our office and he said three more were coming down later after work.

This guy was singlehandedly filling up our waiting room what seemed like every day. Over the next two weeks this one client brought us 34 new clients. I'd say he was a champion client!

Looking back on it now, if I had "half a brain" right at that moment, I should have taken him back to the office, handed him either a $50 or a $100 bill and looked him in the eyes, thanking him with sincere appreciation.

I know you have clients in your database like this. You just have to give more incentive to find them. (The good ones aren't looking for incentive in the first place. But when you offer it, boy it makes it that much better!)

One of our tax offices set our companies' individual referral record when one guy referred 71 new tax clients in one tax season. (That's one client referring over 70 new people into our business!) When you find your champions, cross their palms with gold and silver just like you would a king!

Offer FREE GIFTS with "high perceived value" to stimulate your Word of Mouth

The secret to being able to use FREE GIFTS as an added promotion is getting HIGH PERCEIVED VALUE gifts at a very low cost per unit.

Offering free gifts "kills many birds with one stone." It helps with your unique selling proposition. It helps get attention in your ads. It helps add to the "pile on effect" so you'll at least get a phone call from your prospect.

Free Gifts do all of these things, but they are NOT the main reasons we use them. **The main reason we use free gifts is to STIMULATE OUR "BACK END" SALES** (OR GIVE EVEN MORE REASONS FOR OUR GOOD CLIENTS TO SEND US REFERRALS!)

It's that simple. We routinely spent almost six figures on free gifts alone.

I understand how much it costs to consistently pick up new clients from EXTERNAL advertising. And I can spend the same amount of money giving these gifts away and get BETTER results in many cases.

And not only were we adding new clients from referrals, but we were "cementing" our client base even more and increasing our client retention to even higher levels!

I've had some tax business owners tell me the free gifts they tried didn't go over so well with their client base. So I asked them, "What did you offer them?" Basically, they didn't offer stuff that anyone WANTED. Don't waste your time if you are going to give "stupid stuff."

For a free gift promotion to work, you must offer stuff that MATCHES up with your target market. If your main clientele are blue-collar workers, then have a $6 socket set ready to hand them. (The perceived value of these sets is over $25.)

You can get wrenches and coolers for the guys and cooking pans, necklaces, and cameras for the women. (I can get all of this stuff at wholesale prices from distributors that specialize in items like these from $2 to $6 to whatever you want to pay.)

If you're not sure about using a free gift promotion, just "test" it the first year. Pick out a few things from a couple of catalogs and see how your clients respond. I can tell you from past experience, a third will not care one way or another. You give them the gift and they walk out with their tax return not really caring one way or another.

Now the next third will be appreciative. They will take some time looking at the options you have for them, and then they will choose and say, "thank you." These are your "on the fence" people that wouldn't normally refer people. But now that you've given them a free gift, you have a much better chance.

And finally, the last third of your client base you give the free gifts to will absolutely love them! They will smile real big, get excited, and say, "I can't believe you are giving me this for free!" They will be your big referral clients. Watch for them as you try and keep track of who might be in your "top 20% club."

Over the years as we've implemented free gift promotions, I've come to notice something. The ongoing repeat clients get used to receiving a free gift and actually ask what the new ones are going to be this year.

(Hey, if the most important thing on a client's mind is what kind of $4 gift they are going to get this year, that's fine with me. If all it takes to get a client coming back is to offer a free gift that costs me less than $5, and I'm getting about $400 in return, then I'll give out all the free gifts you want this year and every year to come!)

I recommend B & F Wholesale System for Free Gift products and ideas.
https://www.maxam.com/

Sales Secrets for the Phone and In Person (Part 1)

Nothing happens until you SELL something!

I will argue the point with some of my "non business minded" friends that "Life is selling ... and everyone put on this earth uses some form of salesmanship every day." (Some people just don't buy into this idea.)

I say, look, you sell your kids on getting up and going to school. You sell your spouse on going out to eat at a nice restaurant this weekend. You sell your employees on taking good care of your clients. If you don't think all of these things have some form of selling in them, then I guess I'm going to have to keep trying to "sell" you on this idea.

Why? The more you understand that everything going on around you is happening because somebody SOLD something, the better off you will be "selling" yourself and your tax services.

Salesmanship counts! Preparing a tax return is one thing. **Selling yourself and your tax services as the "best thing since sliced bread" is even better!**

Your ability to SELL yourself is more important than actually knowing how to prepare a tax return. (I'm living proof of that fact.) And I'll tell you upfront right now, our tax business in many cases was VERY AVERAGE at preparing tax returns, depending on the location and time of year.

Yes, I will readily admit that probably MOST of the tax business owners in my Real Tax Business Success Membership group do a BETTER job than our tax business at actually preparing tax returns!

Why is this important? Because it proves my point again. Sales is more important than the actual technical skill (in our case, tax preparation) in a business, especially a service business! So this means that you, the "skilled tax technician," need to get better at this whole "sales thing," or your tax business will never reach its full potential!

Now I hope I've sold you on being a better salesperson in your tax office. If I haven't keep reading.

Answering the "INBOUND SALES CALL"

Answering the phone PROPERLY in a tax office is one of the most important things you can do to increase sales in your business. I can point to numerous times when we have had the "right" person answering the phones in a tax office, and just because we had one of our better "selling" employees on the phone, that particular office would see an extra "bump" in business that day.

The opposite is true, too. I've seen our tax office have a "not so good" salesperson on the phone most of the day taking calls, and sure enough you could see it in our numbers at the end of the day. This is why we didn't let ANYONE answer our phones unless they were a manager, key employee, or had been specifically trained to sell over the phone. It is that important.

What kind of person is best for answering the phone? Well, I like to start with people that like talking to other people (especially on the phone). If they enjoy "engaging" other people in dialog, they'll usually do well at qualifying a prospect over the phone on the kind of services they are looking for, explaining why our tax business is a good option for the person, and then using some simple closing technique. That's all we are talking about. (It's not rocket science.)

There are plenty of people out there that are just naturally good at "persuading" others to follow along with a simple "sales" presentation over the phone and asking them to come to our office and do business with us. They might not know anything about taxes and that's OK. You can find plenty for them to do other than the actual preparation of taxes.

If the person answering your phones can LISTEN to the caller, ASK A QUALIFYING QUESTION and then CLOSE THEM, then you've got yourself an excellent phone sales person!

One bit of arithmetic for you to think about:

If the person you have answering the phone "sells" only three more new clients per day that otherwise you use to not get, multiply that by the number of days in a tax season (about 90).

That means a phone person doing "just a little bit better" on the selling side can bring you an extra 270 new clients into your office. Those kinds of numbers can take some tax businesses from an average year to an excellent year all because of the person on the phone.

Am I selling you on finding the right person to answer your phones this year? I hope so.

(By the way, it shouldn't be you. In the beginning it's OK, but you need to be concentrating your efforts on overseeing "everything," not just on one task like answering the phone.)

Sales Secrets for the Phone and In Person (Part 2)

Make sure you "ask for the order" and close the sale!

This is such a simple thing and there is NO high pressure about it! Most tax professionals don't use any of the regular, "proven to work of over time" sales closes at all.

The four basic sales closes to use: **ASSUMPTIVE, ALTERNATIVE, "PUPPY DOG"** and the **RISK REVERSAL** close.

First, let's talk about the close that "**assume**" the sale. This is an easy one. You just assume every person who ever calls your office wants to do business with you. (There's no doubt about it in your mind or even in your tone of voice.)

Many times the prospect just goes right along with you as you "walk them right into doing business with you" instead of someone else. It just seems like the right thing to do since you are so confident about it.

Your word choices change from words like "if" you come to our office to "when" you come to our office. Another example of assuming the sale would be, "Our parking lot can get full sometimes so when you come today, look for spaces across the street, too." Or, "By the way, my name is Karen. When you come in ask for me, and I'll get you one of those discount coupons I was telling you about."

The **alternative** close is simply giving your prospect two or three choices. You don't care which one they pick as long as they choose one of the alternatives. (Choosing one of your choices means you've made the sale!)

We used this close more when we took appointments for our white-collar target clients. After we had qualified them over the phone and given then the specific reasons why we are their best option to have their taxes prepared, we tried the alternative close on them:

"Now Mr. Jones, it sounds like you need some professional help with your taxes this year. Did you want to try and come in tomorrow or is a Saturday appointment better for you?" Another example would be, "Mr. Jones, we are really busy today. Did you want to wait about a half an hour in our lobby this afternoon, or will setting up an appointment later on in the week be better for your schedule?"

The "**puppy dog**" close works mostly when you are first starting out and you don't have a lot of clients yet. You can make a bold promise in your advertising and then back it up with this kind of close.

Your ad says, "I guarantee your satisfaction with my tax services or your money back!" And when the phone rings you can "puppy dog" close them by saying, "Look, I'll prepare your taxes for you up front and I'll bill you in thirty days. If you don't like my services, I don't want you to pay me!" (It's effective, especially if you need clients.)

And finally, the **risk reversal close**. (One of my favorites.) We usually used this right up front in our advertising. We'd run a headline that says, "I guarantee you'll be satisfied with my tax services or I'll give you all your money back, plus a $20 bill for your time and trouble!"

This reverses all the risk right onto me. So the prospect calls on the phone and practically reads my headline back to me, and I say, "Yes, you don't have anything to lose and $20 bucks to gain! Do you want to come into my office today or is tomorrow better?" (That's assuming the sale and giving an alternative close at the same time!)

Use what works best for you, but USE a close when you are selling your prospects on using you as their tax professional!

A few more "quick tip" sales techniques to use in your tax office:

There are many hundreds (maybe thousands) of sales techniques out there in the sales world for you to "take" and apply to your tax business. Here are a few of my favorites that we used in our tax offices.

- <u>Make your tax office "pleasurable" for your clients.</u> You have heard of the "WOW Experience" Tom Peters has made famous. Well, along those same lines, try to make your office as pleasant an experience as possible.

  Example: A DVD/TV in the lobby for kids to watch videos. Offer snacks, candy or drinks for clients having to wait. Offer discount coupons from area merchants within walking distance of your office. Those clients having to wait over forty minutes can go shop and "kill some time" and not lose their place in line. Set up deals with your "business neighbors" before tax season starts.

- <u>Prepare a list of "negative objections" before your client uses them.</u> You should know ahead of time what possible objections your target client might have about some of the services you offer. Play "devil's advocate" with your own tax office. Why? Because you want to have your answers ready to overcome the objections when they come up.

  Example: Over the phone, the prospect says, "Your prices sound high." You can overcome the objection by saying, "We will never be the lowest price in town, but I'll guarantee you we are cheaper than H & R Block or any CPA in town."

- <u>Keep all of your SALES MESSAGES as simple as possible.</u> Clarity is important. Being easily understood will help you sell more tax services. Whatever you do, **DON'T GO INTO A LONG DRAWN OUT, COMPLICATED "SPEECH"**

EXPLAINING YOUR TAX SERVICES. Keep your selling phrases short and sweet while you are on the phone or with a client in person.

Example: Say, "We prepare MOST tax returns in the same day," instead of saying, "We prepare some tax returns while our clients wait. Others if they are more complicated take longer and we have to get them reviewed. Oh, and if you don't have all your information ready, well we won't be able to finish the return in one day and ..." (In the beginning when you are trying to SELL someone to use your services, stick to your "selling script." You can always explain the details later once the person is SOLD on you being their tax preparer.) I've found this area is consistently one of H & R Block's biggest "Achilles' Heels." Take advantage where appropriate.

- Be "down-to-earth" as you provide "professional" services. Nobody likes dealing with a "know-it-all, ego on wheels!" Just be yourself with your clients. Down to earth and being a REGULAR person is good when you are preparing someone's tax return. Being a "regular guy" that happens to know a lot about taxes is a good selling position to be in.

  Example: Look at how well Dave Thomas (former spokesperson for Wendy's) did. His low key, regular guy approach sold a lot of hamburgers! Don't be a "stuffy and stiff" tax professional. Loosen up and make a friend while you are preparing the return!

These are just a few extra sales techniques we used to increase our business while talking on the phone or speaking with a client in person. We used them because they consistently helped us prepare more tax returns than our competition down the street!

Strategy #43

Your "Bread and Butter" Services

You must have at the top of your consciousness the main services your tax business provides that puts "food on your table." If you are not CLEAR IN YOUR OWN MIND what your main services are, this will cause multiple problems.

Not only will you NOT be able to adequately target the right market for your services, but your message to them will not match properly because of the uncertainty in your own head. If you don't KNOW what you do well, or you are not concentrating on ways to find more people that want what you are good at, your overall marketing plan will be weak and ineffective.

Maybe the biggest hazard to watch out for when you don't know where most of your money flow comes from would be TIME COMMITMENT. If you are spending most of your time helping clients with services that are bringing in the fewest amount of dollars, you need to take a step back and reevaluate your priorities!

I see some tax business owners trying to make extra money in the tax business by offering other simple services on the side. They offer copying services, package and shipping services, and even notary services. The problem with all this extra stuff is it spreads the "small tax business operator" out too thin. They end up spending 40% of their time for net profits at the end of the year, equaling less than 5%!

This is a TIME allocation problem and should be reevaluated! You think you are making more money because your gross sales have increased. But you are not looking at the bottom line. Your annual net profit could be increased if you "dumped" those services and used that same time learning how to market your existing "bread and butter" services more effectively!

If I'm talking to you on this one, go look in the mirror and admit it. DUMP your time wasters and start weighing the "opportunity costs" you are missing out on!

Strategy #44

Leading Employees For Bottom Line Profit

As your tax office grows over the next few years, you will be forced to delegate more and more. Delegation is a good word, contrary to the popular belief that "when you delegate something, it always gets screwed up!"

This is true for those who don't know how to delegate properly. Most owners DUMP assignments on their staff and hope it works out alright. This is NOT delegating; this is a problem waiting to happen!

When you give something for someone else in your office to do, you always have to follow up at the beginning, middle, and end (depending on your working relationship). Don't EXPECT them to get it right if you are NOT INSPECTING the work along the way.

No, that doesn't mean "I might as well just do it if I have to inspect it all the time." That would be foolish.

If you think you HAVE TO DO IT ALL, then the sad reality for your life will be that your business will not grow, and you will be chained to your office forever!

Once you understand this, your business will grow bigger, and you will be able to spend less time ACTUALLY WORKING and more time doing something else you like to do.

But here's the key point:

NEVER STOP INSPECTING YOUR EMPLOYEES' WORK,
or you can expect to get burned in more ways than one. As soon as

your employees "think" you are not watching what they are doing, they will slack up. It's only human nature.

Here's a good rule to evaluate any business decision you make. (When I have not followed this rule, I have gotten burned.)

"IF YOU CAN'T HOLD IT ACCOUNTABLE BY MEASURING SPECIFIC RESULTS, THEN DON'T DO IT!"

That's true for your advertising, hiring new employees, adding a new service to your business, and any other decision that comes up in your daily work life. (If you can't measure its effectiveness, don't do it -- PERIOD.)

Here's another good rule:

Put it in writing, no exceptions.

I've found over the years that if I don't put something down on paper, I'm not really serious about it. That means putting my goals in writing. It means putting instructions that I want followed properly in writing. I even put a "statement of understanding" on a piece of paper for temporary employees just so they are clear about what they have been hired to do.

That goes double for regular employees. They would sign a "non-compete" agreement before they started working with us, but they would also get one of these statements of understanding sheets, too.

Why make such a big deal about putting things in writing, like goals, instructions or employee expectations? Because if you are serious enough to want to make these things run smoothly, you should make sure they get communicated properly.

The problem stems from this "human" thing. We all make mistakes. And usually the first place mistakes happen are because of "communication" errors.

I could say something as crystal clear as Rocky Mountain spring water, but my employee would swear they heard me say something totally the opposite! It happens. So if I don't want to get into any "misunderstandings" with my staff, my vendors or whoever, I'll put it in black and white!

Just for the record, **reducing communication errors or cutting down on misunderstandings within your tax office will MAKE YOU MORE MONEY.** I can look at the "stupid" mistakes we have made over the years that have cost us the most money, and 90% have something to do with a communication breakdown.

I figure I save my business over $10,000 per year cutting down on communication errors. And that doesn't even include the better employee relationships that come from reducing misunderstandings about pay, etc. (I lost a few "good ones" in my early years because we miscommunicated about salary.)

Don't just think these are good ideas -- start "putting it in writing" today!

Another important rule:

Hire SLOW and fire FAST!

This principle applies to every business, but especially in the SEASONAL tax industry. Our tax business hired every kind of employee imaginable over the years, and we have probably made every kind of mistake known to mankind.

Back in the early years, I was the one driving to different cities and doing the interviewing and hiring. Heck, if they were a warm body I was hiring them. But I learned some painful lessons! By not screening "just a little bit" there was much hardship (and lost sales) when employees didn't show up for work, didn't take care of our clients and in some cases blatantly stole from us.

Hey, when you are new at doing stuff, you make mistakes; learn from them and move on. But I'll tell you right now, if I could give all tax business owners one piece of advice, it would be to hire slow and fire fast when dealing with employees! (Especially for the first time.)

You will make mistakes interviewing people and managing them when you are first starting out. That's fine, just take it slow. Find and hire the good ones. Don't just take the first person that walks in your office. (Even though we've gotten some solid employees over the years doing that because sometimes you can just tell someone is going to be good. But when you're not sure, keep looking!)

I also can tell you this. If you have an employee that just is not "getting it" and you have already given him or her multiple chances to get better, do yourself and them a favor; tell them this is their last day and mail their paycheck to them as soon as you can. (Yes, you are doing them a favor, too, because maybe the "firing" will shake them up a bit and make them a better employee for the next business owner.)

Most people don't want to hurt anyone's feelings by firing them. Look, you are not running a popularity contest. You are running a professional business. If they can't cut the mustard, it's not fair for you to make your other employees pick up the slack and not fair for your clients to have to deal with incompetence!

Which brings me to another point: Having "dead weight" employees working in your office hurts your overall office morale, which will definitely cut down on your tax office's ability to offer EXCELLENCE, which, as you know, is extremely important!

Put this "secret" phrase on your wall or at your desk to remind you of its importance as you put together your team this tax season: Hire slow and fire fast.

It's Now or Never

If we all lived in NOW time, procrastination would not be a word. There would be no meaning for it. We would do everything when we thought about it instead of saying, "I'll get to it later." We all know when "later" is. Too many times it's NEVER!

So how do you apply this "now time" principle to your tax business? Well, if you are reading this manual right now in the "off season," I'd be jotting down ideas and things you can do today as well as stuff you want to do before the tax season starts.

Too often tax business owners (including me) put off until the last minute what they know they are supposed to do before tax season. Now the holidays are here and, what do you know, tax season is here again, and you didn't get your list done like you were supposed to.

The secret to getting things done is doing them in NOW time. That means whatever you have on your list to do today, do them now, not later today. If reading these steps is on your "to do" list for today, keep reading it all day. Don't quit and put it off until tomorrow!

"Now time" applies to MAKING DECISIONS, too. How many times have you put off tough decisions just because you didn't want to make it? Being decisive means reacting quickly with reason or a purpose. (Not reacting without reason; that's impulsive and foolish.)

Lee Iacocca once said, "The number one characteristic of super-successful people is their willingness and ability to act decisively."

How come most business owners don't act quickly or decisively?

Maybe part of the reason people don't move more quickly is because of fear. Fear of the unknown consequences. Fear of failure. Fear of confrontation. The bottom line is a lack of "thick skin" plays too big of a role in business owners' lives.

<u>During tax season you have to live in NOW TIME</u>. **YOU MUST CONFRONT PROBLEMS HEAD ON AND SOLVE THEM OR THEY COST YOU MONEY!**

Problems don't usually fix themselves. They usually get worse if you don't deal with them.

Currently, if you're thinking of a problem, I'd go do take care of it now, while you are in NOW time. (It's a good habit to get into.)

Wanna Leave The Country?

Does the thought of leaving your tax office for the whole season with just your employees to run it (and your livelihood on the line) make the hair on the back of your neck stand straight up? How about your stomach? Is it in knots as you imagine what would go on?

It shouldn't be, because you should spend every available minute of your time **systemizing your office so it will run like a top WITHOUT YOU EVER STEPPING FOOT IN THE DOOR!**

This is the ultimate way to run a business. No matter where you are now in your tax business, you can start "delegating yourself right out of a job" today! This is what I did for years and eventually freed myself from the everyday tasks of running the business. I took the responsibility for getting more clients in the door (as should every business owner).

Many tax business owners don't like entertaining the thought of this. Why? Because their self worth is tied up in their work. They think if they don't prepare tax returns, then something is wrong with them. If they aren't busy during tax season (or stressed out), then they really don't feel good about themselves.

Those are self-image and self-esteem issues. (You gotta deal with those things yourself.)

The bottom line is you did not get into the tax business or decide to own your own company so it would control your life! You want your business to serve you, not you serve your business.

Too many tax professionals are chained to their desks every tax season because they have not taken the time to systemize their office so they could have a little freedom!

Michael Gerber says in his book, *The E Myth* (I highly recommend it by the way), that you should systemize your business so well that you could sell a franchise to other people in your industry on exactly how to do everything in your office at exactly the right time.

Example: Have you ever seen a McDonald's franchisee manual? It's the most systemized, detailed thing you have ever seen in your life! (Burger cooked for 92 seconds, then flip, etc.)

What if your operations manual in your tax office was the same way? Wouldn't you feel better about being out of the country for the whole tax season?

A good way to start "working up to this" is to plan a few long weekends AWAY from your office DURING TAX SEASON. This will help motivate you to "get your ducks in a row" better for your employees. (No phone calls either. The building is not going to burn down with you out of town.)

The next tax season, plan a week vacation during the "slower" part of your tax season.

I really mean DO THIS! You ARE the owner. (You can take off anytime you want.)

As you get more use to doing this, your systems in your office will become better. You will have more and better quality "key" employees "watching the fort" for you.

Decide now what your ultimate goal is and plan your systems around it. If it's leaving the country for the whole tax season, while your business takes in a six figure net profit (and you never stepped foot in the office the whole year), then do it!

The Way You *Really* Get a Flood of Clients

It's smarter to use fifty different ways to get one client, than one way to get fifty clients!

In marketing, diversity is the opposite of laziness! In the long run, it's better to know fifty different ways to bring a new client into your tax business than to put all your eggs in one basket and try and generate the same numbers with one ad.

And you know, it's actually EASIER to learn fifty "little" ways to get one new client at a time as compared to "hitting a home run right out of the box" with your first ad.

So how come more tax professionals don't learn the "little easy" ways to land more new clients? It's called MARKETING LAZINESS! (I admit, it is much more fun to write one ad that'll bring in a bunch of new clients right off the bat. But the reality is I built our tax business on MANY marketing ads, picking up ten to fifteen clients at a time.)

Yes, we've had our share of "BIG HITS" when close to 200 people responded to one little third-of-a-page flier (half of them new clients). But you don't always get those kinds of responses, so in order to play it safe, you DIVERSIFY!

Does finding fifty ways to get a new client overwhelm you? It shouldn't. Just go by this simple rule during tax season and you will not fall into the "marketing laziness" trap most tax professionals do.

Starting January 1st, don't let a day go by without trying or testing one simple promotional idea. By the 50th day (or the middle of

February), you will have found over a dozen (probably closer to two dozen) ways to get one or two clients at a time.

Let's say you have found twenty ways to get at least one client every time you do them. That's POWERFUL! And you will not be doing most of these marketing ideas now. You will have delegated them to your staff or hired high school kids to do them after school.

What kind of ideas am I talking about?

1. A small classified ad (both offline and online) that gets three calls every time you run it, and one of those three comes in to have their taxes prepared. (The ad costs $50 and you make $300 or net $250 each time it hits the newspaper.) Switch headline if response slows, and retest again.

2. A high school kid promises to hand out (at least) fifty coupon fliers door to door every day after school, stamping a red deadline date at the bottom validating your "special offer" good for only the next ten days. You pick up one new client every time this kid hits the streets. That's five per week (or $1,500) and you're paying him an hourly wage totaling $50 to $100 for the week.

   (This is also a good way to find "hungry" neighborhoods starving for a quality tax service business.)

3. You do a deal with the owner of a pizza business. His delivery people take a copy of one of your full-page ads and staples it to their pizza boxes. They deliver 800 pizzas per week to local homes and businesses around your tax office. Three clients respond per week, by bringing in the ad with a pizza stamp on it. The deal you made gives the pizza owner was he'd get $25 per new client you receive. He gets $75 per week and you are netting $825, plus you are picking up three new clients each week for free with no effort.

Are you catching my drift? These are easy ways to pick up one or two clients at a time. Once you get them up and running, they run by themselves, or you have other people run them for you from your office.

No, it's not flashy. No, you are not going to get your picture in the paper for the biggest response ever for a single ad.

Depending on how aggressive you are, you'll have fifty or more new clients coming into your tax office per week, netting you large sums of income. This is how million dollar tax businesses are built, one client at a time!

(It might not be a story for Hollywood, but I don't think the bank tellers will refuse your money when you bring the deposit down to your local branch.)

Timing Is Everything

Do you know when your target markets are the "hungriest" for your tax services? Do you know when they are more likely to call you, come by your office or take some kind of action that commits them to your tax business? How about the WORST times to promote to your target client? (That is even more important sometimes, since the "window of opportunity" in the tax business is so small.)

Timing in the tax business can mean everything. (When a bear is starving, it doesn't matter too much what kind of food is in front of him at the time. He's just gonna eat because he's HUNGRY.)

The same can be said about your target market(s). You feed a "starving crowd" when they are hungry. Like the bear, once they have eaten, it doesn't matter after that. (In our case, it doesn't matter for a whole year later.)

So knowing your sales cycles before tax season begins and planning your marketing campaign around those "selling windows" is the best way to go.

From early February to February 15th there's a lot of people who've just gotten their W-2s and are thinking about their taxes. Maybe you've sent them a reminder in early January about taxes this year, and they're now getting all their 1099s and W-2s in the mail.

This is a great time to test and run ads (for a white collar target market). Why? Well, mainly because they are getting tax related documents in the mail all the time now. But more importantly, most other tax businesses mailed their sales letters back in early January and have NOT sent any follow-ups.

IF YOU SEND OUT A SECOND OR THIRD MAILING IN
MID-FEBRUARY, YOU STAND A GOOD CHANCE OF
"PITCHING" YOUR SERVICES WITH LESS COMPETITION.

If you are mainly in the electronic filing bank product business, you know you need to get clients in your office as early as possible! If you want a piece of the refund loan market, you've got to advertise in early January to early February (or you miss this lower income market.) These folks want their money now, and as soon as they get their W-2s, they are often in a tax office that very night!

I think every tax business should go after both the blue-collar, low-income market and the other higher-income target clients because the timing is so different that you CAN do both!

Final Words

"YOU CAN'T EAT EFFORT!"

I don't know where I heard that, but I like it and it's very true.

People in the business world get caught up in "being busy" too much. They confuse EFFORT with RESULTS. They think that just because they are busy or they've got a lot "going on," they are successful.

This is especially true in the tax industry. Just because you are "busy" during tax season or you have a lot to do doesn't mean you're making more money or that you are improving your tax business.

What kind of effort is better? Concentrated Effort that gets results is far better than just running around like a chicken with your head cut off!

Personally, if I get in the office and write a couple of solid ads for a promotion that's coming up, and it takes me two or three hours of uninterrupted time to do it, that's a much better use of my time than to stick my head into some "everyday" problems that our staff can handle just as well as I could.

I prioritize. I decide what's the best time for me. I concentrate and focus when I work and seek to reach my goal of successful, measurable results at the end.

Now what's more productive and better for you and your business in the long run?

Working a few hours in the morning, focusing your time with concentrated effort (and then taking the rest of the day off) or just being in the office handling whatever problems arise (and putting in a long day at the office)?

Another good question is, how do you "practically" GET STARTED and begin developing habits of efficient and concentrated effort?

One way I've learned is once I hear or think of a good idea to implement, I immediately write 'down an action plan for that day and the next few days to implement it (right then and there) -- "Now Time"!

You see, another secret to getting things done or implementing all the good ideas you get in any given week, is to ACT as fast as possible on the ideas that you feel warrant the HIGHEST priority!

THE SPEED AT WHICH YOU ACT ON A GOOD IDEA IS EVERYTHING! After that, all you are doing is ATTACHING TIME to the priorities you feel are important!

If you want to succeed, find and follow "mentors" who have gone down THE road you want to travel!

It's very rare to see any successful individual get to wherever he or she has gone and NOT have some kind of mentor or coaching relationship with someone who has been there before.

Anyone wanting to succeed in specific areas of their life needs to seek out and find mentors in those areas. I have one or two marketing mentors I continue to study and learn from. It is an area of my life that I want to get better at and succeed at even more.

Mentors can't DO IT for you, but what we can do is help you cut down on a lot of normal mistakes and pitfalls that come with the territory. Since we've been down the road you want to go, we can save a lot of time, money, and effort!

Besides getting coaching from me, you should also find a local mentor in your community that you can meet with on a regular basis. It can act as your ongoing "accountability, kick my butt into-gear" sessions.

Hey, if it helps to get you to take more action, then by all means, meet with some local business people and let them "kick your butt into gear!"

Just a little bit more" can make a huge impact in your tax business!

"In the land of the blind, the one-eyed man is king!"

Erasmus of Rotterdam
Renaissance Philosopher

If everyone in the tax industry is walking around "blind" to the real ways of promoting and selling tax services, by using these Strategies from my Tax Marketing Crash Course, you have become "just a little bit better" than your competition.

How do you think that will affect your bottom line?

If you work at being just a little bit better, your bottom line will show a huge improvement in profit! Why? Because the tax business client doesn't pay you for second place. You either get the sale, or you wait until next year.

If you are a little bit better at getting your prospects' attention in your ads, if you are a little bit better at getting a potential client to call you, if you learn to sell a few more people over the phone to come do business with you rather than someone else ...

THESE LITTLE THINGS MEAN MUCH MORE PROFIT!

It does not take much to be a little bit better than others in the tax industry. Just act on a few of the Strategies in this Tax Marketing Crash Course and you'll become a little bit better -- I promise!

Little stuff like: writing a headline, having a deadline, including a call-to-action or coupon in your ad, using testimonials in your promotions … even systematizing your office paperwork just a little bit differently, which helps you become more efficient so you can produce more tax returns and handle a high number of clients in a day.

These are all simple examples that, applied to your business just 10% better, could make as much as a 50% net profit on your bottom line.

(And that's nothing to sneeze at!)

And finally, a tribute to you:

You made it through my 49 Crash Course Strategies.

You WILL get "a little bit better" this tax season and beyond as a result.

Who knows where you'll be a couple years down the road?

Regardless, keep me posted and in the loop on your progress.

All the Best,

Chauncey

Feel free to pass along the online version of this Crash Course to other tax business owners outside your market area. We have compiled these **"49 Tax Marketing Lessons"** into one place for your convenience:

https://taxmarketing.com/49-lessons

What Tax Business Owners Should Do Next

Chauncey Hutter, Jr knows no one can predict the future with complete certainty. Depending on when you are reading *Crash Course*, changes to the tax industry could be at one extreme or another.

So, as a tax professional, here's your best next step moving forward. Go to this website and add your name and contact info.

www.taxmarketing.com/crash-course-next-steps

Someone from Chauncey's Real Tax Business Success staff will send you the latest info on how you can benefit from the changing landscape of the tax industry.

If you stay ahead of the curve, your chances of beating your competition increase dramatically, and your opportunity to build significant wealth goes up, as well.

Stay tuned and up-to-speed with the latest and greatest ways to grow your tax business profitably in these uncertain times.

Claim Your Free Copy of Chauncey's
Amazon Best Selling Book

BLOCKBuster: How to Build
a Million Dollar Tax Business

book.taxmarketing.com/order-book-free

Real Tax Business Success
205 2nd Street SW
Charlottesville, VA 22902
(434) 293-2707
chauncey@taxmarketing.com
www.taxmarketing.com

Made in the USA
Columbia, SC
16 May 2018